PEOPLE & in CORNWALL

MICHAEL WILLIAMS

BOSSINEY BOOKS

First published in 1985
by Bossiney Books
St Teath, Bodmin, Cornwall
Designed, typeset and printed in Great Britain by
Penwell Ltd., Parkwood, Callington
Cornwall

ISBN 0 906456 97 5

PLATE ACKNOWLEDGMENTS

Front Cover of Sir John Betjeman by Jonathan Stedall
Back Cover of Penny Barrett riding across Trengwainton Carn by Ray Bishop
Ray Bishop: pages 5-7, 12-19, 29, 32, 56-62, 66-69, 74, 81-83, 90, 92, 96-103
Richard Hawken: pages 8, 20-27
Bryan Russell: pages 28, 42, 44, 47, 51
Gloucestershire County Cricket Club: page 70
George Ellis: page 11
Richard Angove: page 31
Alice Boyd: page 37, 46
Ronald Youlton: pages 78, 80

ABOUT THE AUTHOR—AND THE BOOK

A Cornishman, Michael Williams started full-time publishing in 1975. With his wife Sonia, he runs Bossiney Books from a cottage and converted barn in North Cornwall—they are literally cottage publishers, specialising in Westcountry subjects by Westcountry authors. For ten years they ran the Bossiney House Hotel, just outside Tintagel—hence the name Bossiney Books.

Outside publishing and writing, Michael Williams is a keen cricket enthusiast and collector of cricket books. He is President of the Cornish Crusaders Cricket Club and a member of the Cornwall and Gloucestershire County Clubs. He is also a member of the RSPCA, and has actively worked for reform in laws relating to animal welfare. Recently he was elected to the Ghost Club, and remains convinced Cornwall is the most haunted area in the whole of Great Britain.

In *People & Places in Cornwall*, Michael Williams writes about ten people who, in their different ways, contributed richly to the Cornish scene. They are the former Poet Laureate, Sir John Betjeman, at Trebetherick; Marika Hanbury Tenison, writer and explorer of Bodmin Moor: author Denys Val Baker who lived in a fascinating collection of homes all over Cornwall; England cricketer Jack Crapp who was born at St Columb; sculptor Dame Barbara Hepworth and potter Bernard Leach of St Ives; Rowena Cade who created the Minack Theatre; the internationally famous Cornish painter Peter Lanyon who was based in Penwith; Wallace Nichols, the poet of Penzance; and Frederick Glasscock who became an Arthurian legend at Tintagel. 'It is,' says the author, 'a star-studded cast, and their lives, individually and collectively, remind us of Cornwall's genius to fire the imagination . . .'

Introduction

Writing these pages has been like trying to exorcise a ghost or, more precisely, ten ghosts. The idea of putting together ten different people who have contributed vastly to the Cornish scene has haunted me for some years—long before the comparatively recent deaths of three of them.

All are now gone but I had the luck to meet eight of them. Sir John Betjeman, though a Bossiney author, I never met—yet curiously we did speak. It was our first winter in North Cornwall. Sonia and I were visiting some old cottage ruins at Port Quin, one Sunday afternoon, when I ventured upstairs and called out to Sonia, who wisely stayed below, 'Nobody's lived here for years and years.' 'You're quite wrong,' called out that famous Betjeman voice. 'I can remember families here only a few years ago. Good afternoon!' And the man, who was to become Poet Laureate, continued his stroll up the lane.

Of the remaining eight, I met all and all eight, in varying degrees, made a considerable impact. But outside and beyond that, in their lives they underlined Cornwall's genius to fire creativity.

All ten who parade these pages were creators, 'givers' in Life. Even the one businessman created something very remarkable at Tintagel and though Jack Crapp was a professional cricketer, due to the influence of Sir Neville Cardus (whom I did meet), I rate most cricketers as 'artists'. A batsman, who scored a century against Bradman's Australians, *must* surely have been creative.

One day at Morwenstow Ronald Duncan told me that a man who lives twenty five thousand days or so, will, if he's lucky, remember 'not more than a couple of hundred at the most'.

Right: St Enodoc Church is the heart and the soul of Betjeman Country in Cornwall.

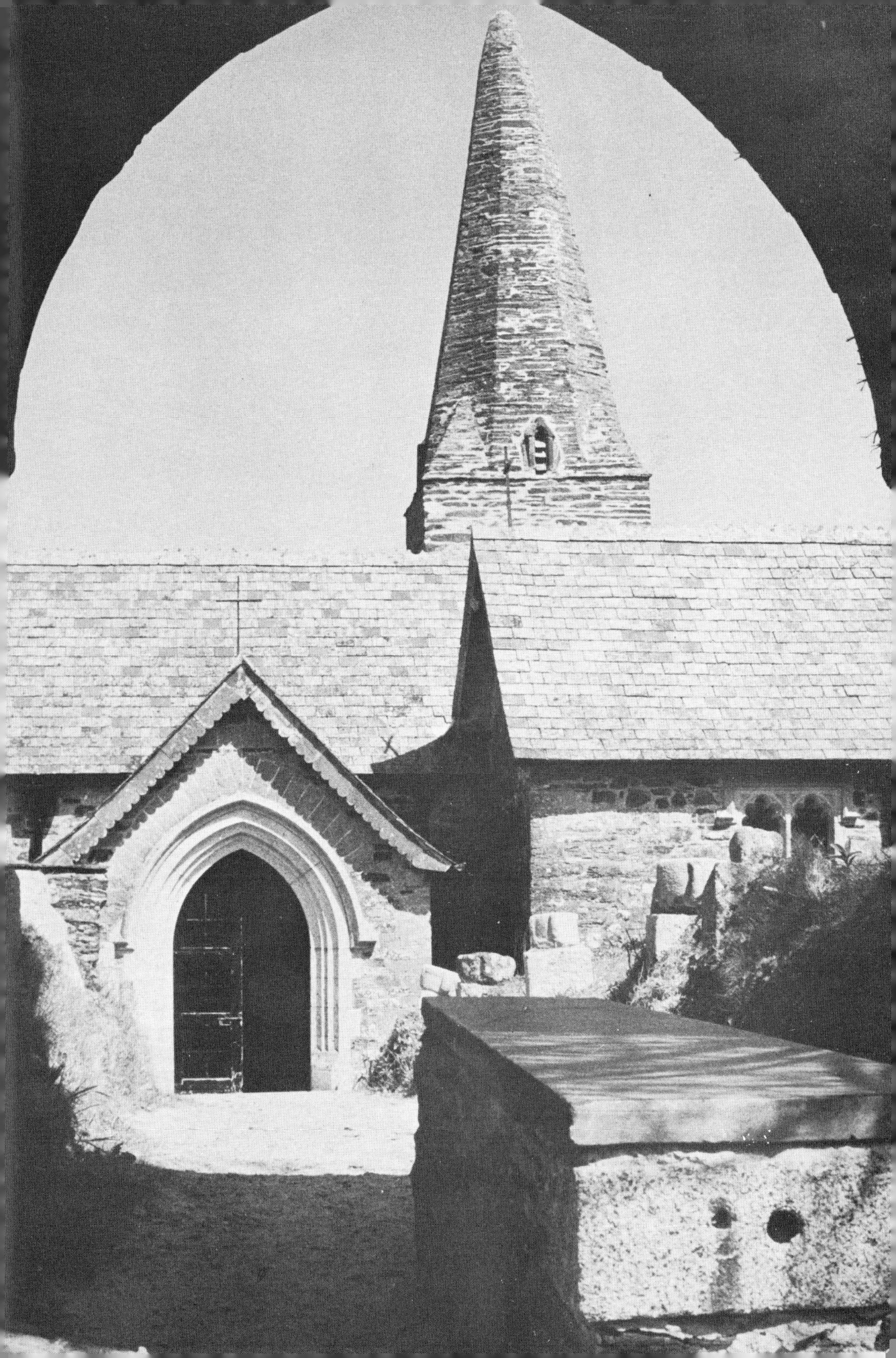

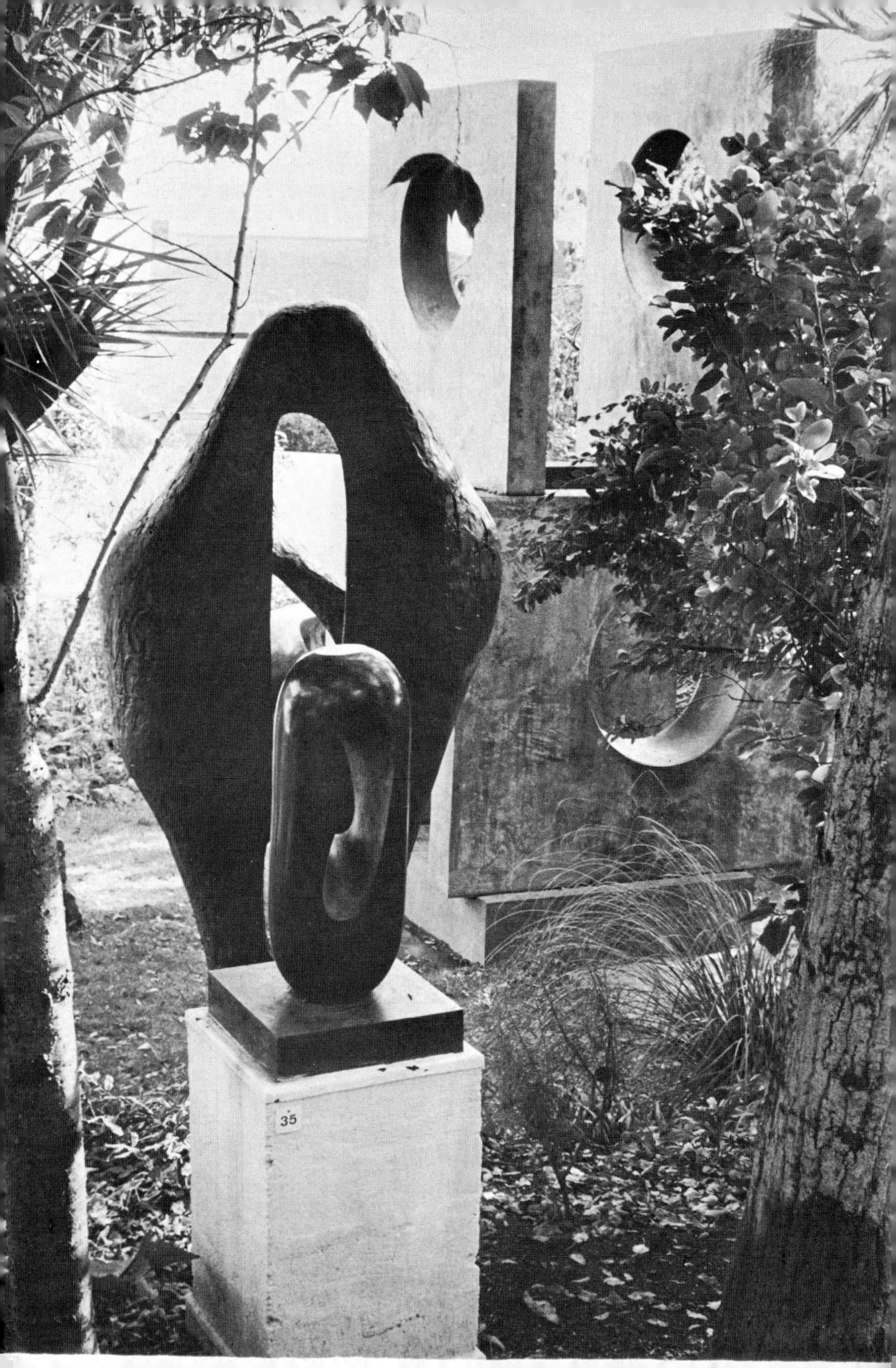
35

Some of the meetings with the people featured in the pages that follow will be among my two hundred.

The snide critic will accuse me of name-dropping because these ten chapters are about ten very different, very distinguished people.

Sometime, I'd like to write about some of the less-famous who have been an influence: my old tutor Edmund Sedding, the most absent-minded character I ever met; Jerry Sweet, a wonderful Port Isaac fisherman who supplied us with fish at Bossiney for years and firmly declined to go 'decimal' believing 'it'll never catch on'! Even after decimilization, Jerry still gave us our bill in pounds, shillings and pence. Then there was my great-aunt Mabel Williams who taught me to read and opened a whole new world, and that great Tintagel philosopher Allen Menhenick. Allen was a County Council work-

Left: Barbara Hepworth sculpture in the garden at Trewyn. Below: North Cornish coast. '. . . remind us of Cornwall's genius to fire the imagination . . .'

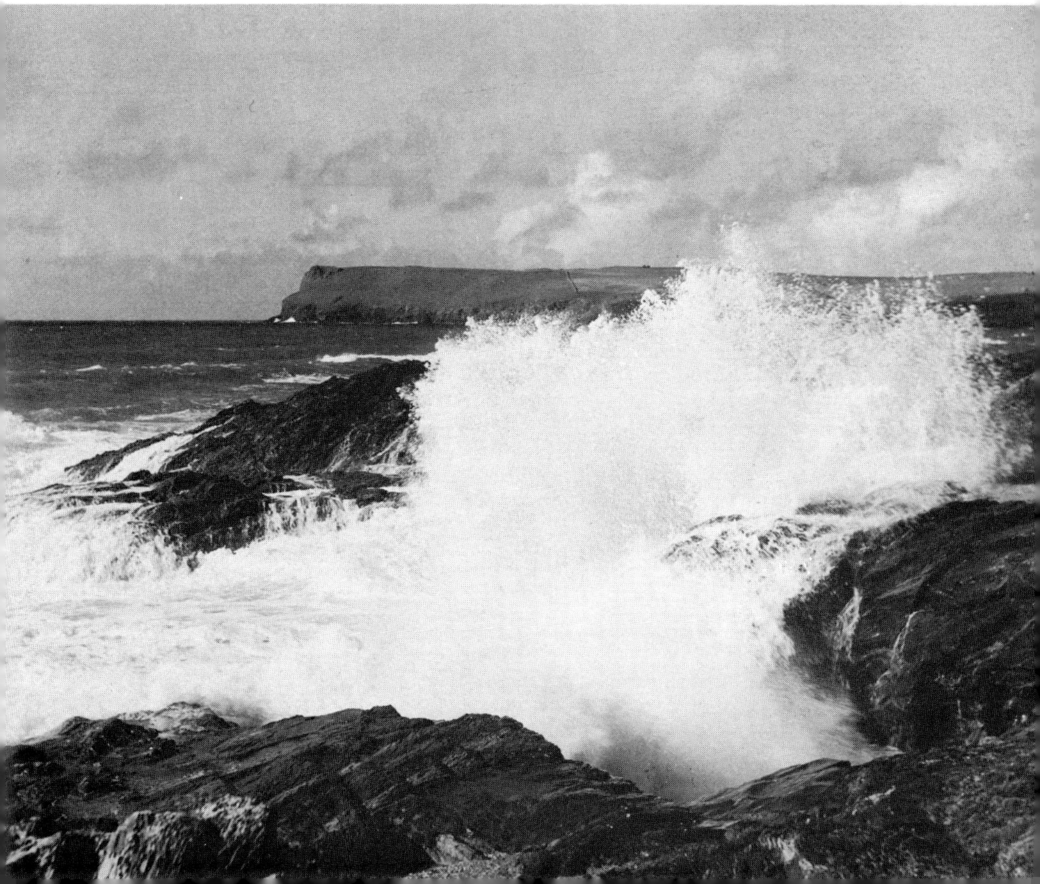

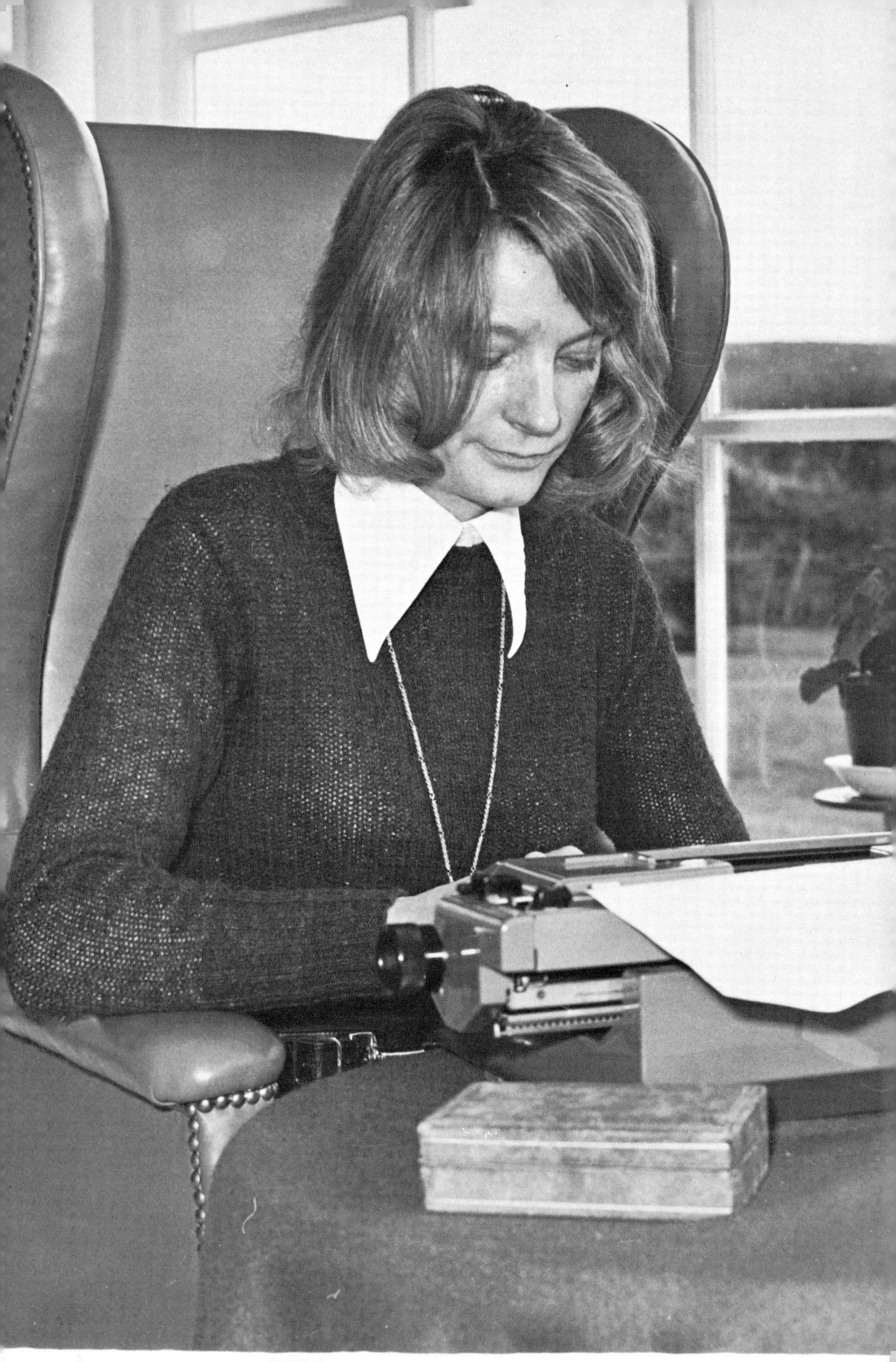

man, but I still rate him a philosopher. Typical of the man was when a holiday visitor complained about the wet weather. 'Look, mister,' said Allen quietly, 'there are lots of people up in Tintagel churchyard who would love to feel the rain on their faces.' Yes, Allen was a philosopher and an incredible fund-raiser for charities. Throughout his life he must have sold hundreds of thousands of raffle tickets for hundreds of charities. Allen deserved a place in *The Guinness Book of Records* and lesser people have found themselves in the New Year's Honours List. Then there was Syd Rice, dairyman, another North Cornwall philosopher and friend of many. But hopefully, one day, their turn will come.

For the present, though, the spotlight falls on the ten in the following ten chapters. Interestingly, only two, Peter Lanyon and Jack Crapp, were natives.

But the other eight, in many ways, were Cornish to the bone—in heart and spirit anyway—and all ten refused to live in a narrow limiting groove.

Shakespeare might have been thinking of them when he wrote: '... in following him I follow but myself.' In following themselves, they were faithful to something way beyond themselves—their stars or their destiny perhaps—and I, for one, cannot believe the thing we call death defeated any of them.

I am sure they only went through a door.

Left: Marika Hanbury Tenison at work in her home on Bodmin Moor.

Sir John Betjeman Trebetherick

The most famous Poet Laureate of all time died peacefully in his sleep at eight o'clock on Saturday morning 19 May 1984 at Trebetherick.

The knight who loved St Pancras Station and trains and disliked Slough—he invoked German bombers 'to mess up the mess they call a town'—had been nursed through a long illness by Lady Elizabeth Cavendish who had been his constant companion for many years.

A frail figure in his last years; Parkinson's disease had confined him to a wheelchair when travelling, enabling him as he once put it 'to play the aged invalid to perfection!' He had a stroke in 1981 and a heart attack in 1983, rallying amazingly, he claimed, through the healing qualities of his childhood teddy-bear Archibald Ormsby-Gore who was rushed to his hospital bedside.

On Tuesday 22 May Sir John Betjeman was buried at his beloved St Enodoc, with its leaning spire, alongside the graves of unknown sailors whose ships had perished on the Doom Bar in the Camel Estuary. It was a simple service—strictly private at the request of his family—the tiny church decorated with wild flowers; oil lamps and candles providing the only light. They carried his coffin between the sand dunes in driving rain, almost gale force conditions—the kind of weather that might have triggered another poem.

The bearers, almost soaked to their waists, were son Paul Betjeman, son-in-law Rupert Lycett-Green, Chris and Ben Harbour, Lord Eliot of St Germans and Jonathan Stedall.

Sir John defied neat easy classification. They called him the

Sir John Betjeman photographed at his home at Trebetherick in October 1972—on the day he was appointed Poet Laureate.

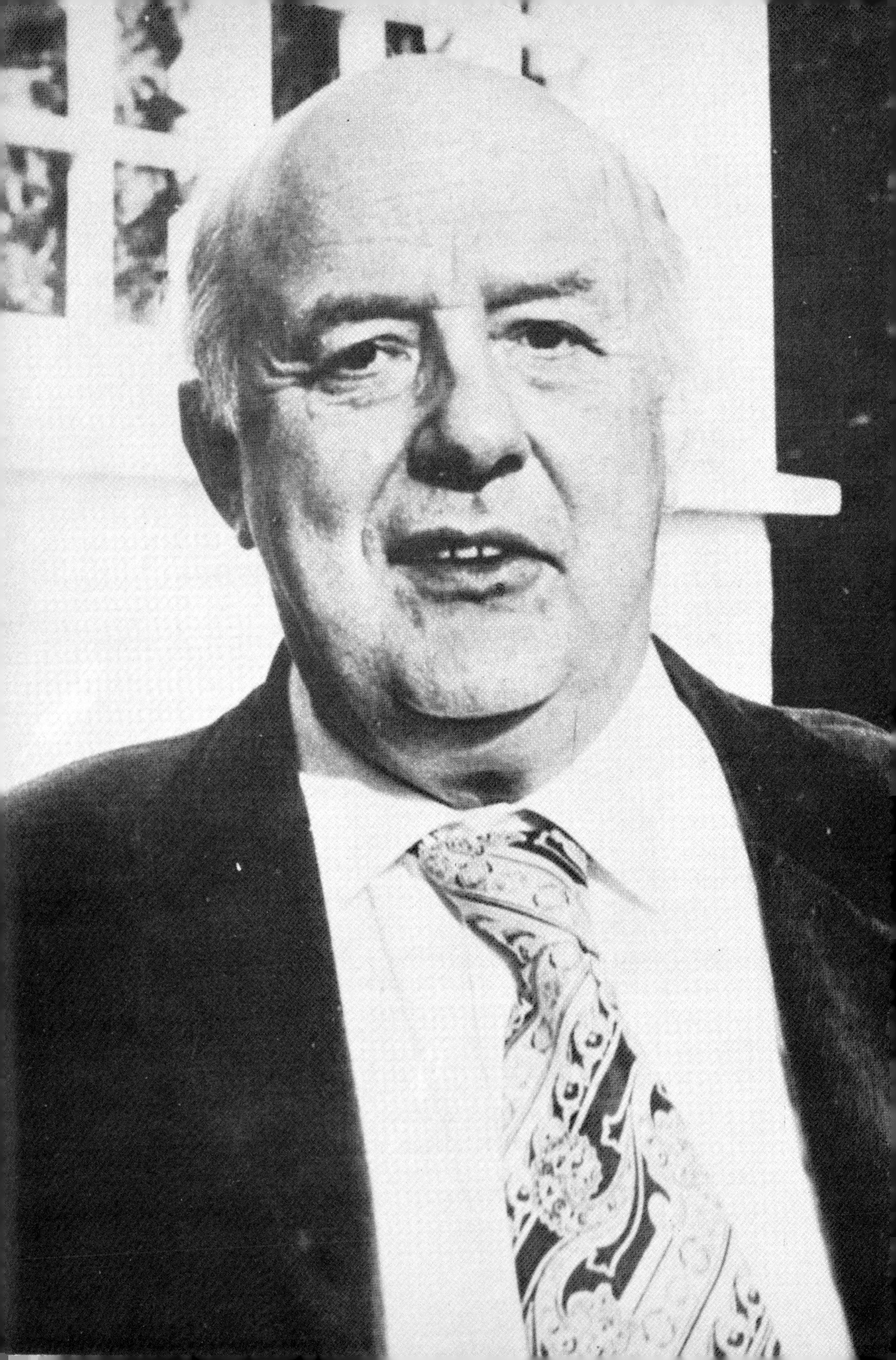

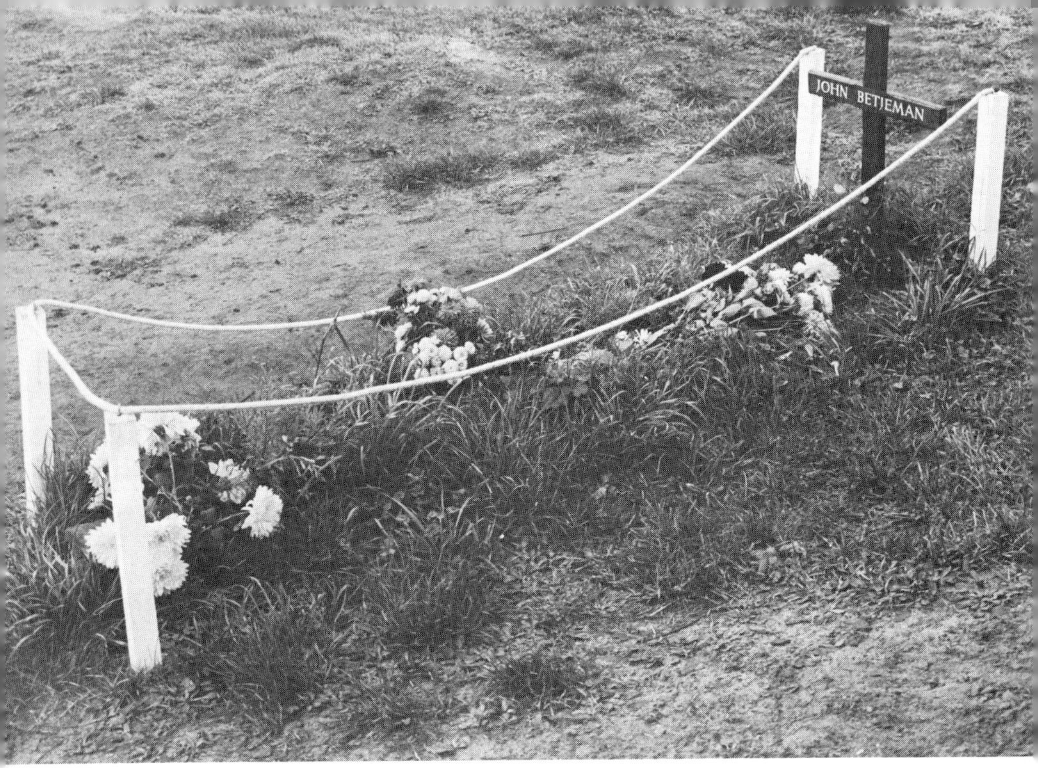

People's Poet, but as Kenneth Young wrote in his obituary in *The Sunday Telegraph*, 'He was delighted to become Poet Laureate, though he was no snob; he just preferred dining with Dukes than with dustmen . . .' It is said he was proud to have once been labelled: 'By Appointment: Teddy Bear to the Nation.'

He was, in fact, a considerable all-rounder: architectural critic, social historian, conservationist, short-story writer, railway enthusiast, countryman, humourist, churchman and eccentric—he was all these—and a good deal more.

In 1969 Denys Val Baker, the Editor of *The Cornish Review*, suggested an interview with Sir John Betjeman would be an attractive idea. I was delighted at the prospect, and wrote off asking the Poet Laureate if he would give me an interview when next in Cornwall.

'Dear Mr Williams,' he replied. 'Goodness knows when next I shall be down in Cornwall, but if you are ever up in London, the above address will find me. I know I'm going to Iceland at the end of January, I thought it would be rather nice there out of season, with daylight for only two hours. I am not a native of Cornwall, but a

Sir John was buried (left) at St Enodoc Church (below) set in the sand dunes near his Cornish home.

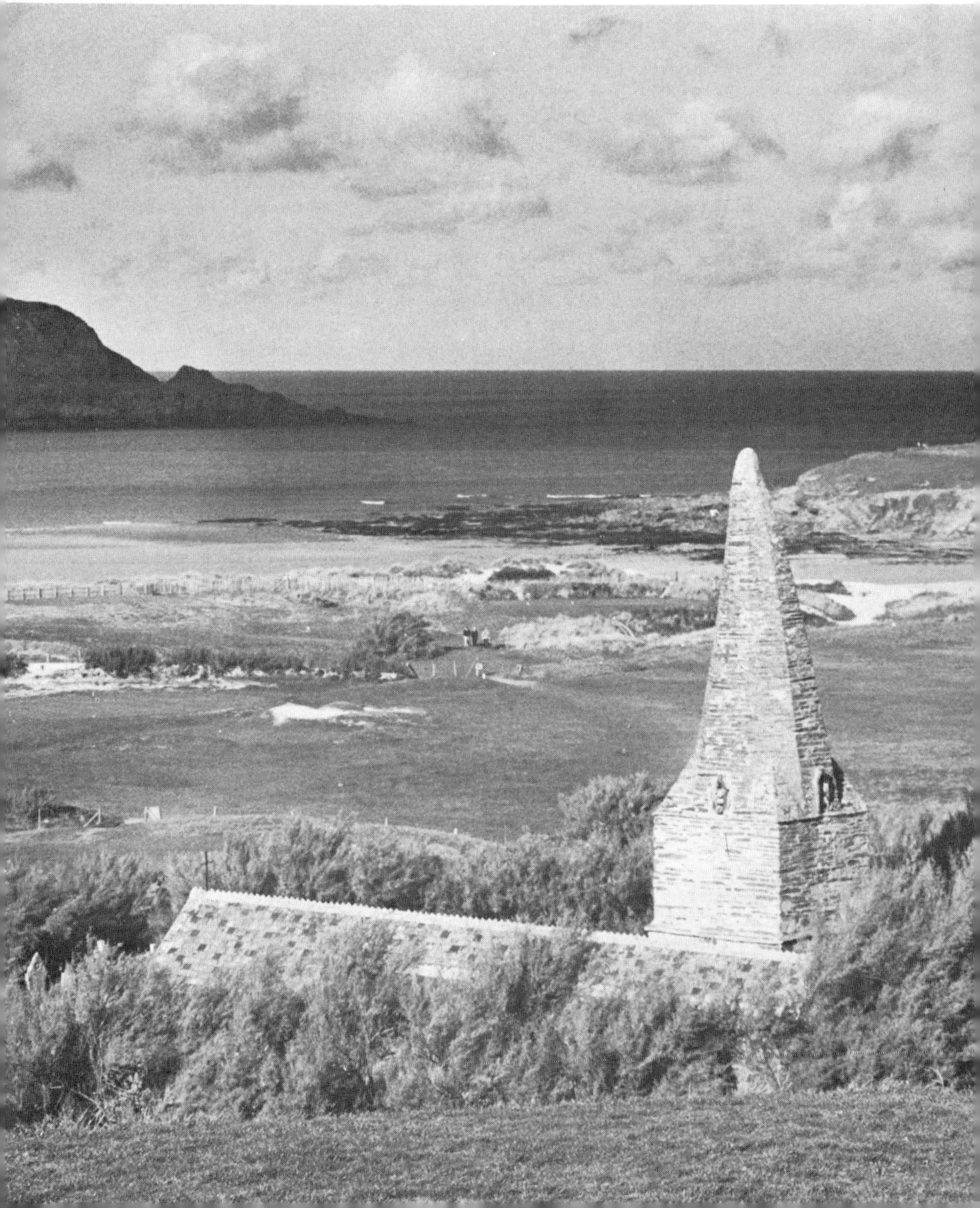

suburban Cockney. With best wishes, Yours sincerely, John Betjeman.'

I didn't think it too amusing at the time and interpreted it as a fending-off reply. Now, of course, I shall always regret the fact that I didn't pursue the matter further.

Even so Fate worked in a mysterious way.

Fact is Bossiney Books have special reason to be grateful to Sir John. Back in 1974, when we had published only a handful of titles, I hit upon the idea of a Westcountry Alphabet—A to Z about Cornwall and Devon by a team of authors. Looking back, I realise it was rather cheeky to ask the Poet Laureate to contribute a chapter.

I did, at least, have the good sense to say, 'I realise we can't pay you what you're worth.' His reply and his chapter came back within 72 hours; 'Here it is . . . this is all I can manage . . . chop it, change it

Below: Looking across the Camel Estuary to Padstow. Right: A golfer on the course at St Enodoc, with the church just below.

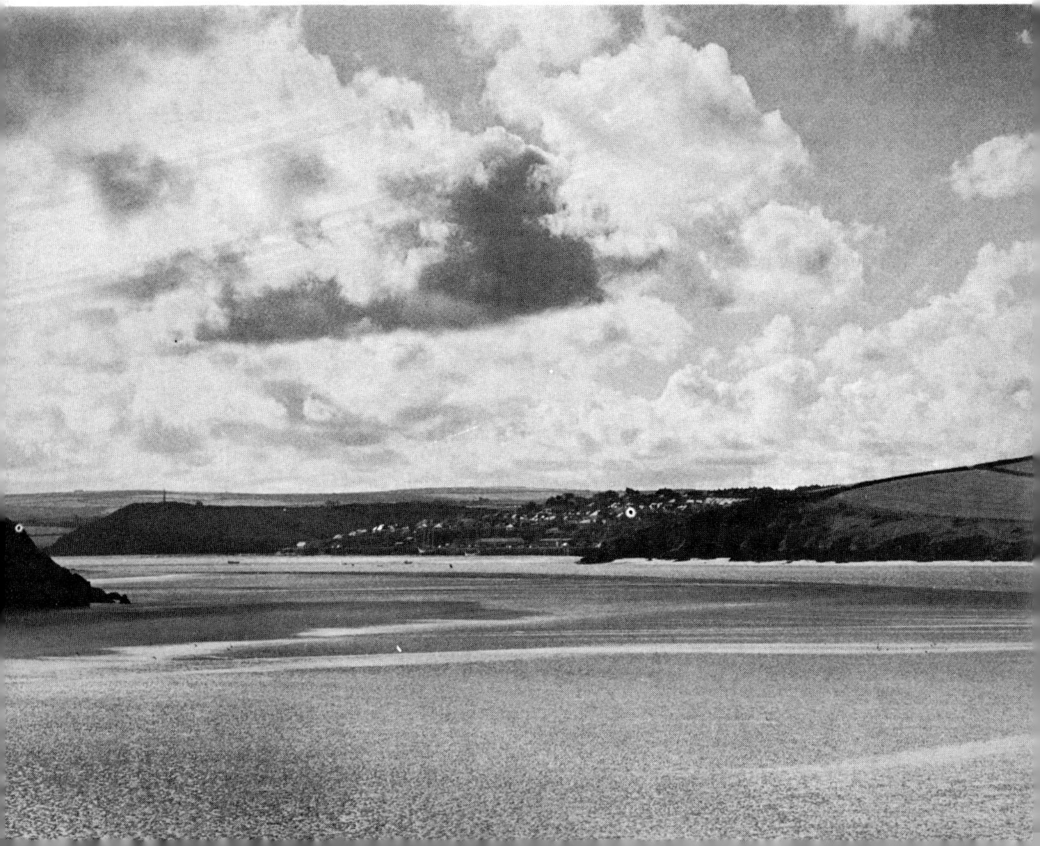

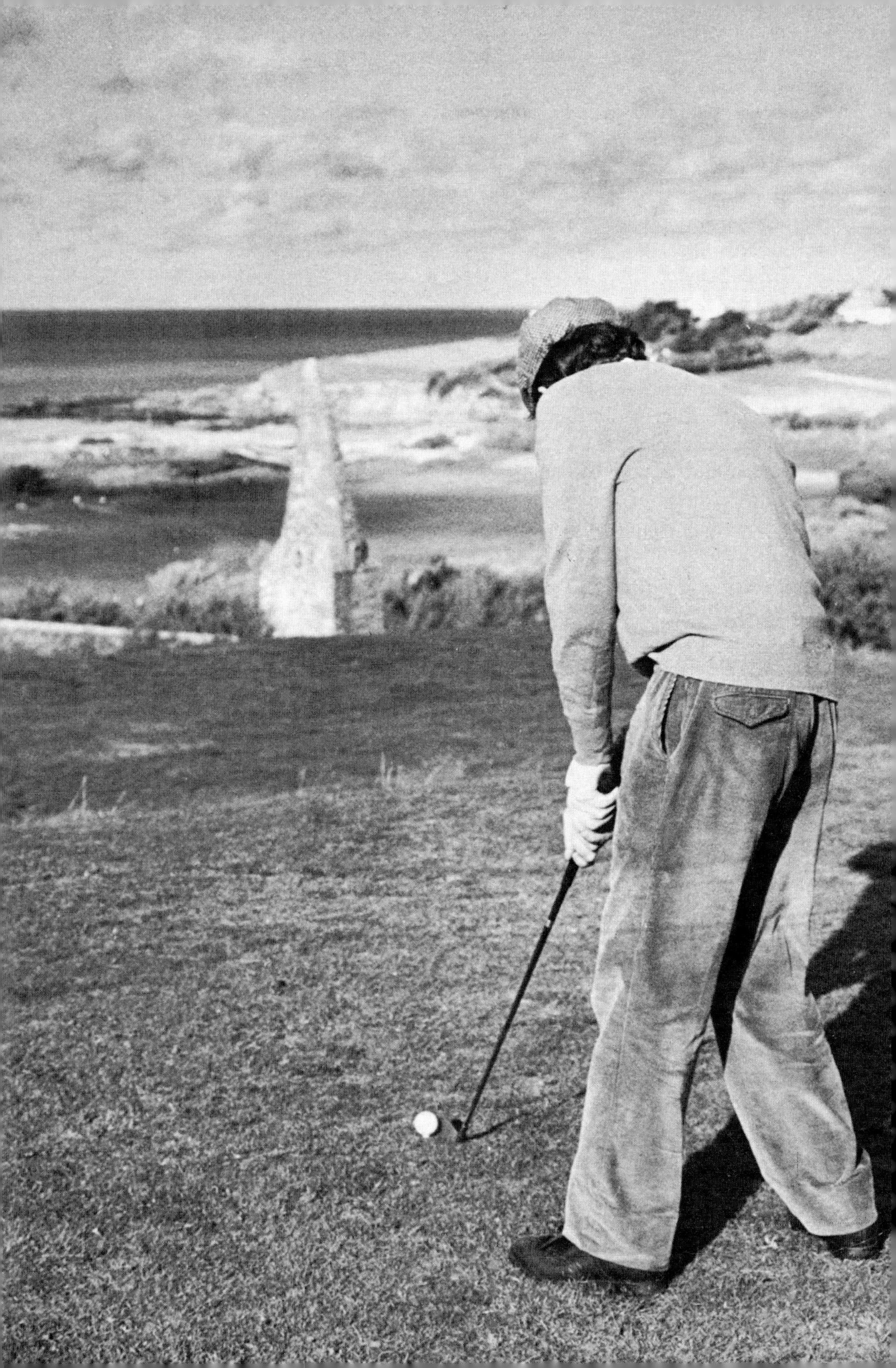

or reject it . . . and only pay me the same you're paying everybody else.'

It was T for Trebetherick, of course, and here is an extract from it: almost certainly the first and last time a Poet Laureate will write for a Cornish cottage publisher.

'Trebetherick . . . it may have been a suburb by the sea and for all our crabbing, fishing and bathing, nothing to do with the real Cornish who regarded us as the foreigners we still are. But for me it was home for the eyes, the nose and the ears. The great, black half-moon of Bray Hill with its three cairns on the top, the long low stretch from Padstow to Stepper Point on the other side of the estuary. The regular cragginess of Newland's rocky island. The changing vegetation of the high-hedged lane . . . all these for the eyes. For the nose there was the scent of seaweed and salty sand. Wild mint at one season, honeysuckle and thyme at another; and drying cow-dung always. For the ear there was the roar on the shore when the tide was high. The utter silence when it was low. The larks and oyster-catchers shrill and small, and sea-gulls wailing like angry babies. The rumble of wooden wheels over stony roads and the far-off puff and rumble of the London and South Western as it crossed the viaduct on its way to the Padstow terminus, the end of that long slow journey of the ambitiously named Atlantic Coast Express.

'This was my Trebetherick.

'Its people are mostly elsewhere. Some in St Enodoc churchyard.'

Sonia and I stood in that same churchyard in May 1984, looking at his grave, the floral tributes still incredibly fresh, but the ink on the cards blurred through the torrential rains. A grey mist hung over the Camel as the foghorn sent out its loud warning tone.

Yet strangely there was nothing sad or sombre in that churchyard, flanked by the beautiful greens of St Enodoc Golf Course. Here anyway, I felt that death was not the end but a door opening. Perhaps a local resident spoke for many: 'In a funny way, we're all relieved . . . he suffered so much.' 'How wonderful that he died here in Cornwall,' said another. In Cornwall, many felt he had come home to take a last look at the land he loved—and to die.

He loved our wide Cornish skies, the beaches and the changing sea, the cliffs and the churches, and, above all, treasured his boyhood memories of a vanished Cornish way of life. He fell in love with Cornwall as a child, and it was a love affair that never ended, for though he wrote movingly of other places in Britain, Cornwall called

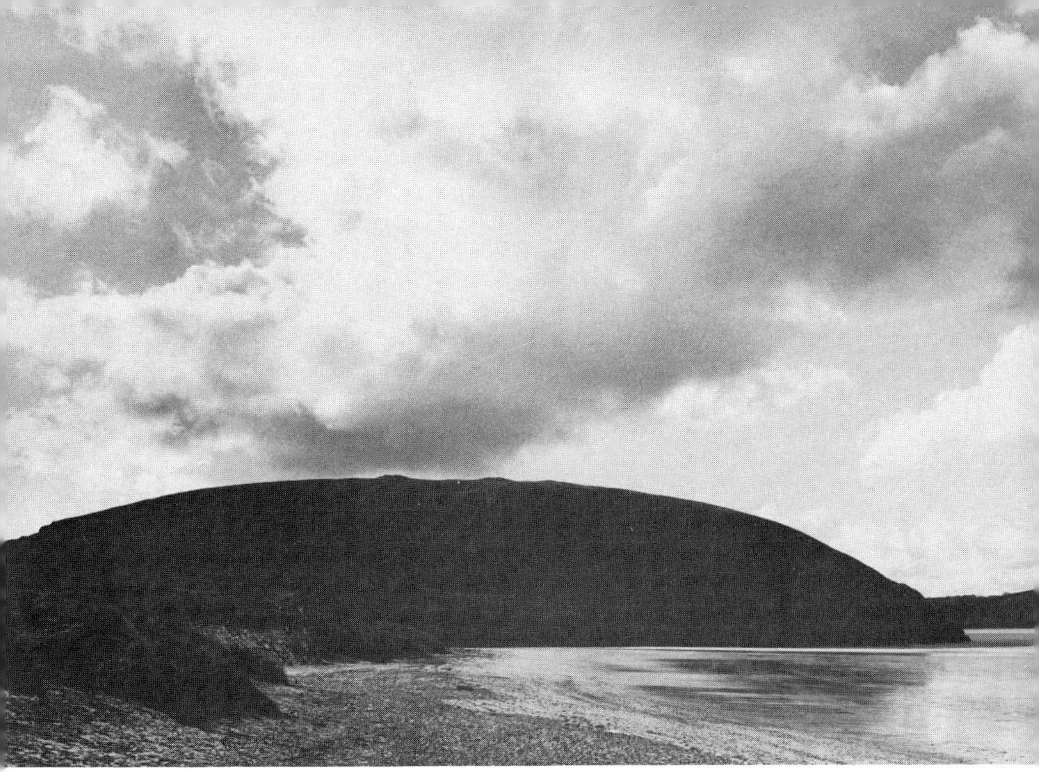

'The great, black half moon of Bray Hill . . .'

him again and again, firing his writing—like a first love that would not let go. Curiously, in the last fortnight of his life, John Murray, his publisher, produced *Betjeman's Cornwall*, a mixture of his poems and prose married to pictures, ancient and modern, and some specially-commissioned drawings by his old friend and collaborator, John Piper. It is a beautiful, evocative celebration.

Cornwall had this tremendous influence on his life: childhood on the sands at Trebetherick, and later golf on this lovely St Enodoc course, Sunday services at St Enodoc Church, a tiny building once buried in sand, and visits to Port Isaac or Padstow across the estuary by ferry, walks on the cliffs, trips inland to beautiful churches like Blisland and Altarnun, tea or a drink with adult friends he had once known as children. Then, in the sixties, he acquired a house at Trebetherick called Treen, almost next to the house his father owned when he was a boy.

How will future historians and critics see him?

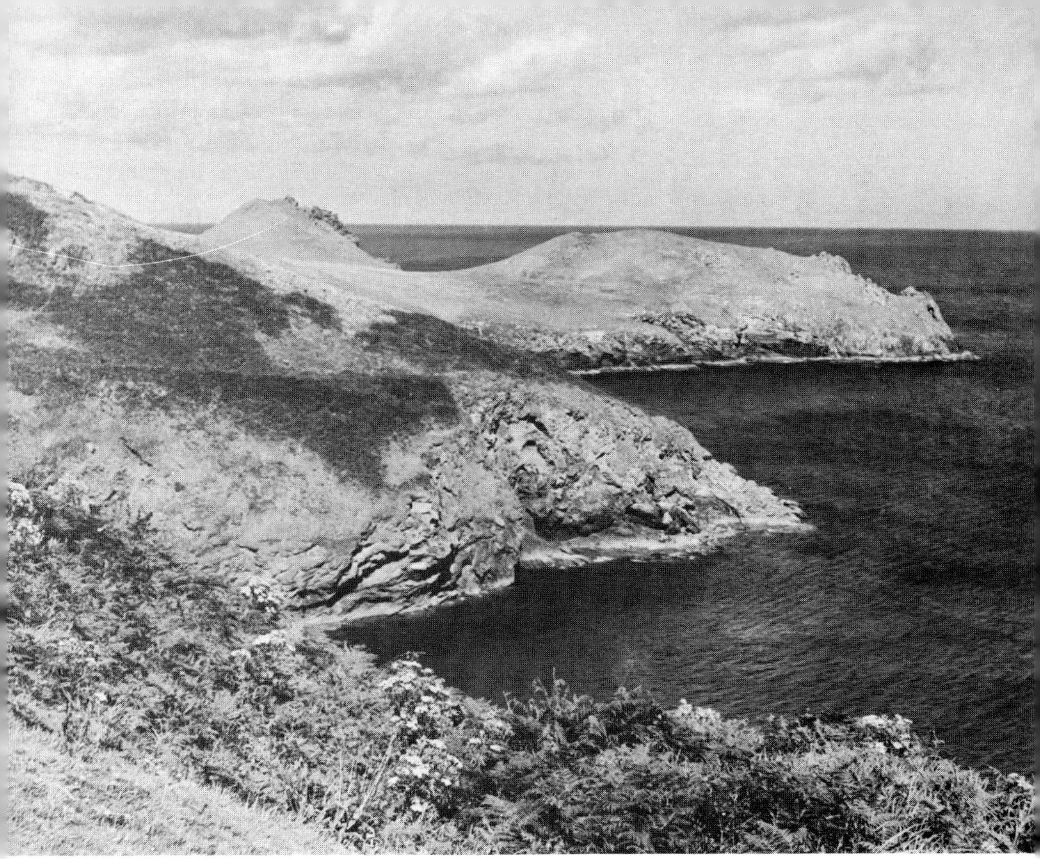

Almost certainly as a literary phenomenon: that very rare bird, a poet and a bestseller. His collected poems, first published in 1958, have sold hundreds of thousands of copies. His television appearances of course helped, and critics will disagree about his work in death as they did in life—forgetting that blame and praise often depend on preference and prejudice inside the critic.

But the Cornish Vicar, the Reverend Anthony Gent, at his funeral probably got to the heart of the matter when he said, 'He brought modern poetry from the esoteric to a level where it could be read with enjoyment by the less highbrow and by untold numbers across the world.'

And what about the man behind the fame and the huge sales? Who better to have a last word than his friend for nearly fifty years, the painter John Piper?

'John was a missionary,' he wrote in *The Sunday Times* the day after Sir John's death.

'He would often ignore a church, a building—even a poem—of great accepted beauty because it didn't need his appreciation. The unloved, the deprived, the aesthetic outcasts were what he went for; but never if they were not conceived in love and in sincerity. He was not, as many people claimed (especially in the early *enfant terrible* years) a lover of the second-rate. He was a lover of the human spirit.'

Two views near the mouth of the Camel Estuary. 'He loved our wide Cornish skies, the beaches and the changing sea, the cliffs and the churches . . .'

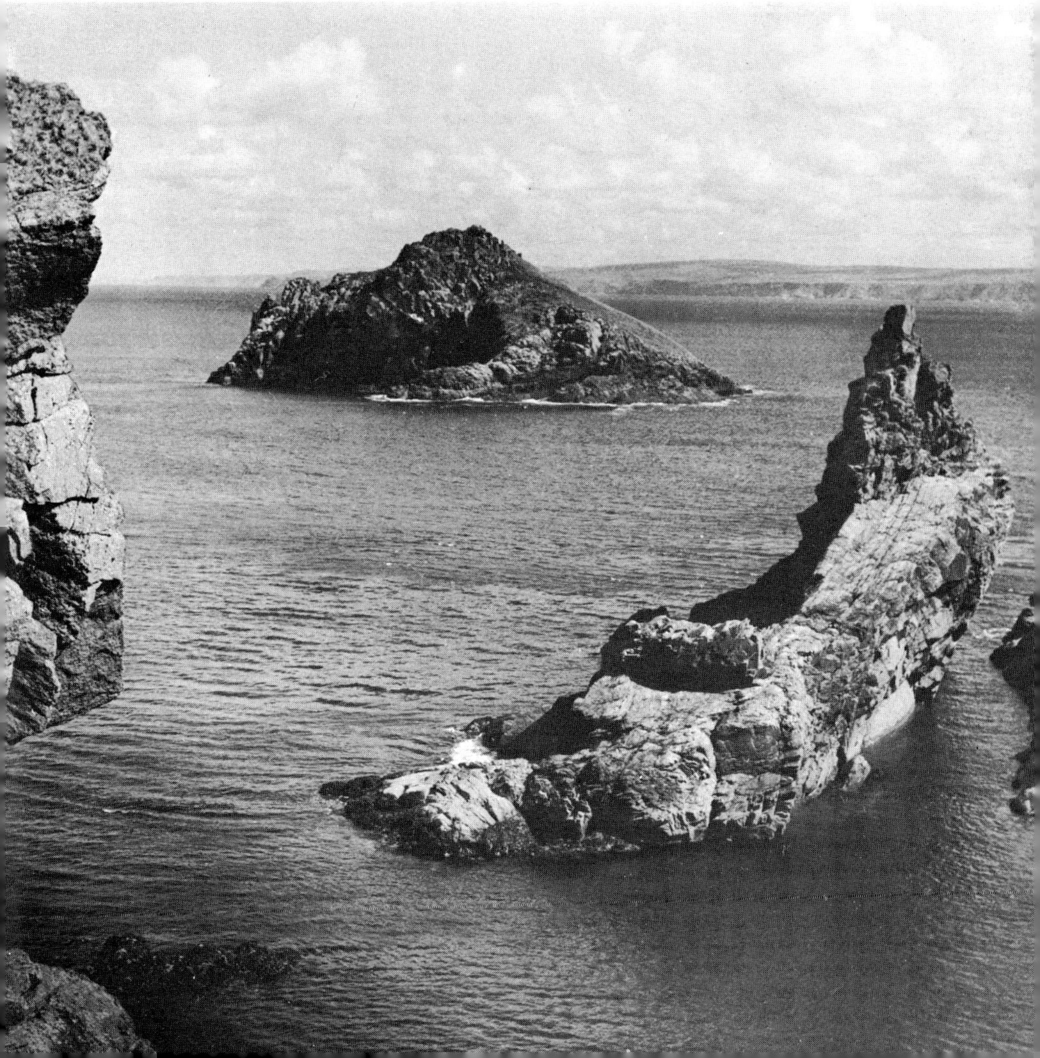

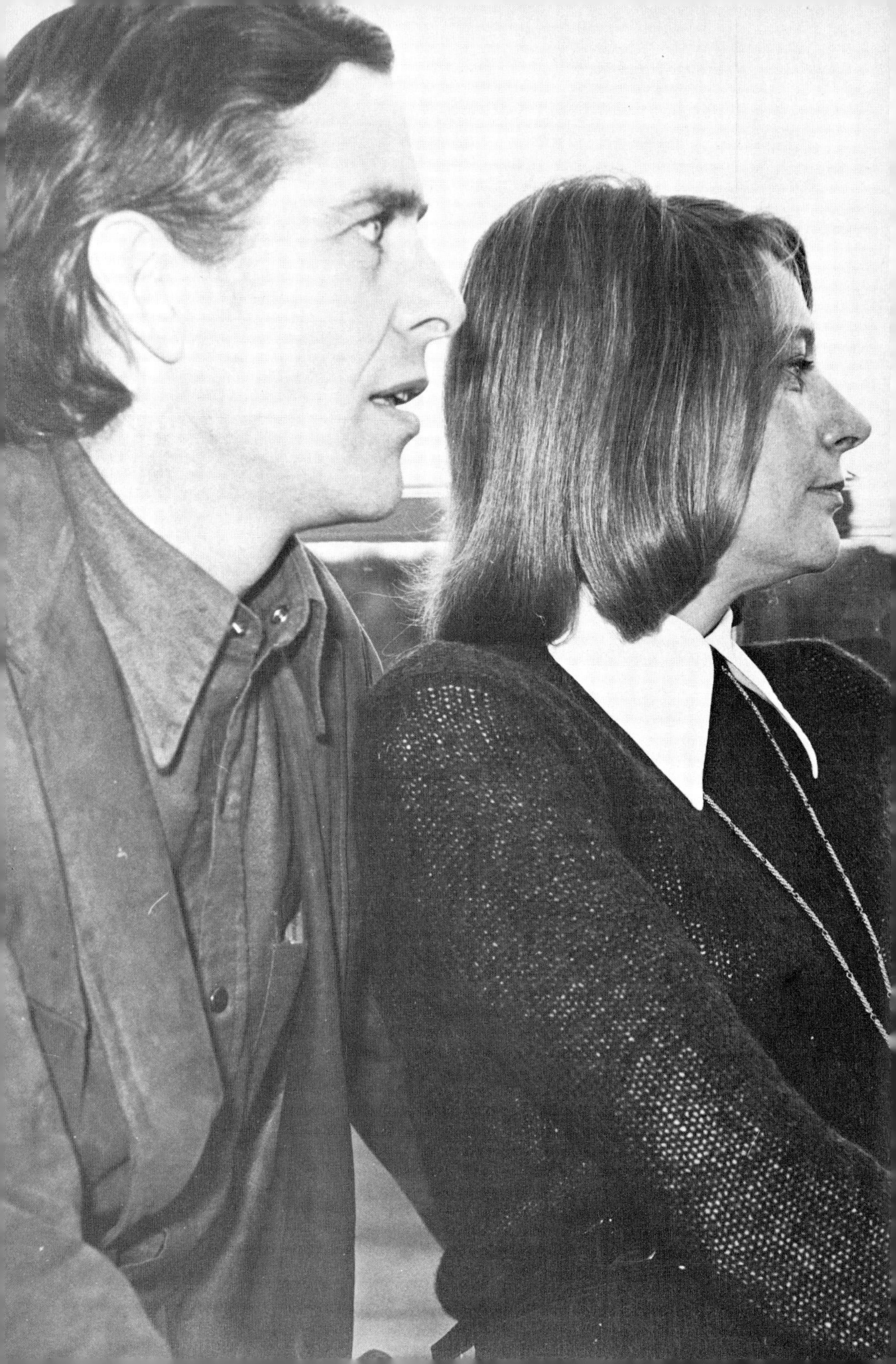

Marika Hanbury Tenison
Bodmin Moor

Marika Hanbury Tenison loved Cornwall and, in a way, was more Cornish than many of the natives. She was a great supporter of Bossiney Books too. In 1975, when we ventured into full-time publishing, she generously contributed to *A Meal for All Seasons.* It was a star-studded list of contributors, containing famous names like Angela Rippon, Rita Tushingham, then living at Polperro, Joan Bakewell and Jean Nichol Tangye among others. It was a commercial disaster, but it helped to establish us as cottage publishers in the Westcountry, and nobody did more than Marika to promote the book. She appeared on local television and wrote about it in her column in *The Sunday Telegraph.*

Here is how she opened her chapter in *A Meal for All Seasons:*

'Occasionally I find myself having to cook for a lunch or dinner party in the kitchen of our miniature mews house in London. Despite the fact that the kitchen there is a model of streamlined design, the process is agonizing and every minute I spend there I long for the space of my farmhouse kitchen on Bodmin Moor, the door that lets the draughts (and the dogs) in from both sides, the Aga that decides at the eleventh hour to misbehave, the gum boots drying on the marble slab, the telephone ringing when my hands are covered with pastry and the crowing of the bantam cocks from the cowshed.

'When I am in London I miss "shopping" in Cornwall too. At Maidenwell, there is a corner of the garden where fresh herbs can be picked as they are needed; in Bodmin a few small shops still battle on against the supermarkets. I can buy vegetables that have not travelled a few hundred miles in a juggernaut and Cornish's Dairy will order special things for me if I give them advance warning.

Left: Marika with her husband Robin Hanbury Tenison.

Along the cliffs we can pick wild spinach, on the estuary dig for clams or prize mussels off the rocks; in the spring I make elder-flower champagne and in the autumn we freeze blackberries. It does not take a few days penance in London to make me appreciate Corn-wall but it does help to remind me just how fortunate I am to live here.'

Those two paragraphs underlined her love for Cornwall. It was a book which deserved to succeed. It failed for a variety of reasons. It was, at the time, competing against many other cookery books. On reflection, we should have gone for a lower price range and backed my original hunch to feature Angela Rippon on the cover, but, worst of all, the marketing was appallingly handled by the wholesalers.

Later I had the miserable experience of writing to all the contri-butors saying 'Sorry the royalties are so poor . . . we're having to remainder it.'

Marika must have known we had lost a fair amount of money on the project, for she never cashed her royalties cheque. I didn't forget that caring gesture because in our first two years of full-time pub-lishing it was, as Wellington said of Waterloo: 'the nearest run thing you ever saw in your life . . .' It was, not to put too fine a point on it: touch and go, and Marika must have sensed that too.

With her explorer writer husband Robin, she came to Cornwall in 1960, to farm on Bodmin Moor. She started writing seriously in 1968, and when I approached her in 1974 to contribute to *A Meal for All Seasons,* she was in the throes of writing as many as three cookery books and at work on her first novel. She also contributed to journals as diverse as *Vogue* and *The Christian Science Monitor, Reader's Digest* and *The Sunday Mirror.* In the midst of all this, she was cookery editor for *The Sunday Telegraph,* and yet she still accepted my invitation warmly and produced her manuscript promptly.

She had already published two travel and adventure books, *For Better, For Worse* and *A Slice of Spice.* Her cookery books, at that stage, included *Soups & Hors D'oeuvres, Leftover for Tomorrow, Deep Freeze Cookery, Eat Well & Stay Slim* and *Marika Hanbury Tenison's Menus for Each Month.* Moreover, she never missed a trick in the publicity stakes; so in addition to her prolific authorship and journalism, she made numerous appearances on television and radio. Producers and directors were ready to co-operate for she com-municated naturally and brilliantly. Her cooking in front of tele-

Cookery editor for *The Sunday Telegraph*, Marika loved the space of her farmhouse kitchen on Bodmin Moor.

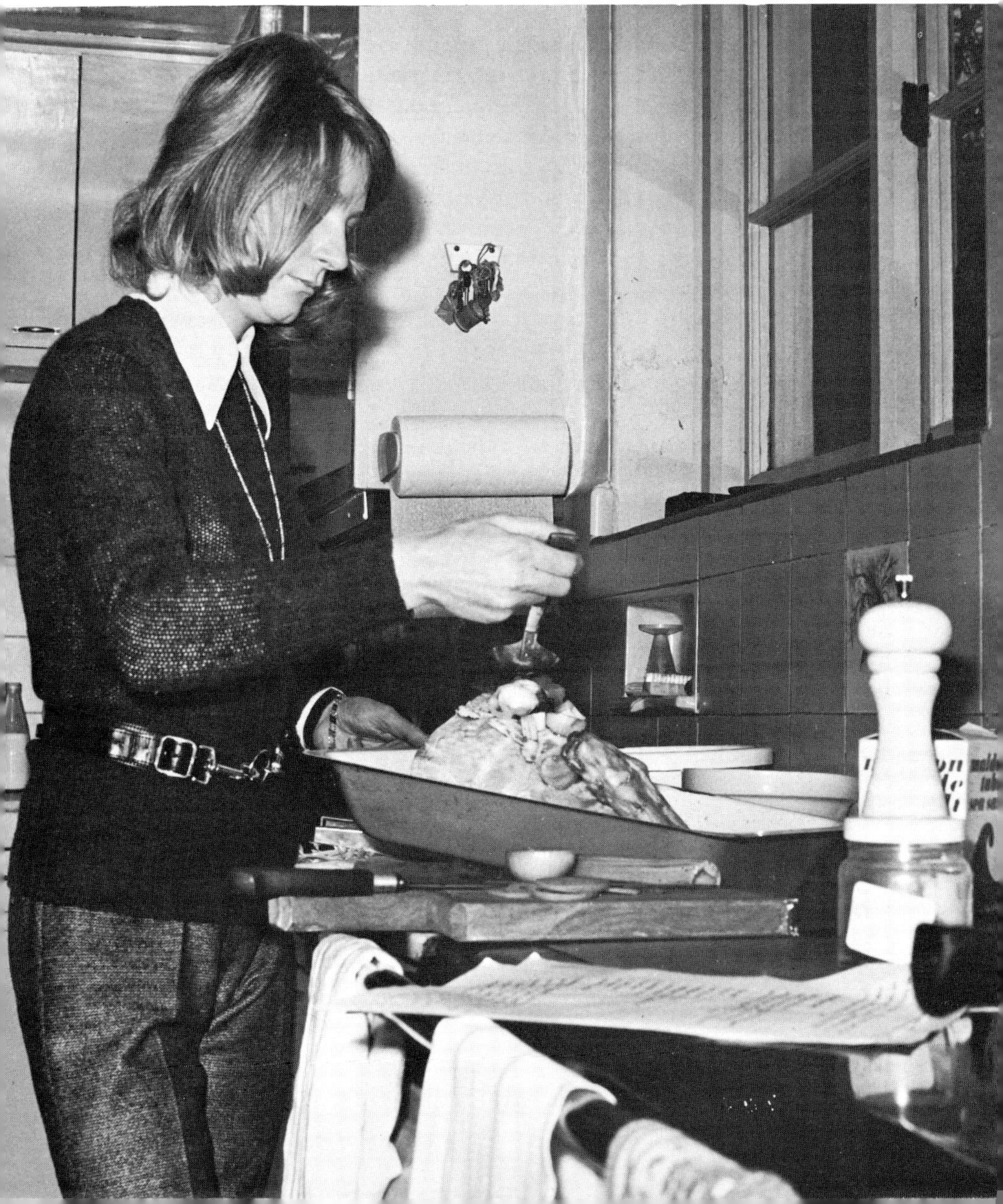

vision cameras was often a combination of education and entertainment.

She had a great regard for Westcountry cooking: 'It has a richness almost unsurpassed in the British Isles,' she once said. Revelling in the access to fresh, natural ingredients of the region—like the shellfish, the flat and deep sea fish, the game in the woods and the mushrooms in Cornish fields—she thought 'Westcountry food had a flair and flavour all of its own'.

I only met her twice, first when she kindly invited Sonia and me to a charity day at Maidenwell. It was a memorable occasion, for apart from the setting and the magnificent food in the open air, it seemed as if half Cornwall was there, and yet she still found time to talk to us and enquire about Bossiney Books. Moreover she seemed to find time to talk and enjoy everybody's company. It must have been an illusion because it would have been physically impossible, but her magic was such that you could believe her capable of anything.

Our second meeting was at a Bossiney authors lunch at The Cornish Arms, Pendoggett. We didn't know for sure, but she was by then desperately ill and only months away from the thing we call death, yet she was full of enthusiasm and interest, positively thrilled we had made such progress since the disasters of *Meal.* Again, we knew she had cancer, that she was virtually serving a death sentence yet she still managed to create the illusion—just as she had mystified by appearing to meet every one of the hundreds who had attended Maidenwell on that earlier occasion.

For the second half of the lunch at Pendoggett, we sat next to one another—her fair good looks she inherited from her Swedish mother—she told me how she thought she'd do some publishing of her own at one time, but finally ran into distribution problems. The books were apparently made in such a way that they wouldn't burn, and 'we ended up burying hundreds of them at Maidenwell!' Only someone with her zest for life could have told such a story turning publishing tragedy into pure comedy.

About three years earlier she had been told she had cancer and went with Robin to Mexico in search of a cure—it was a costly exercise and failed to produce the answer. Coming back home, facing certain premature death, Marika retained her remarkable energy and vitality to the end.

In the hope of helping fellow cancer sufferers, she made her serious illness a public matter by appearing on BBC TV: a pro-

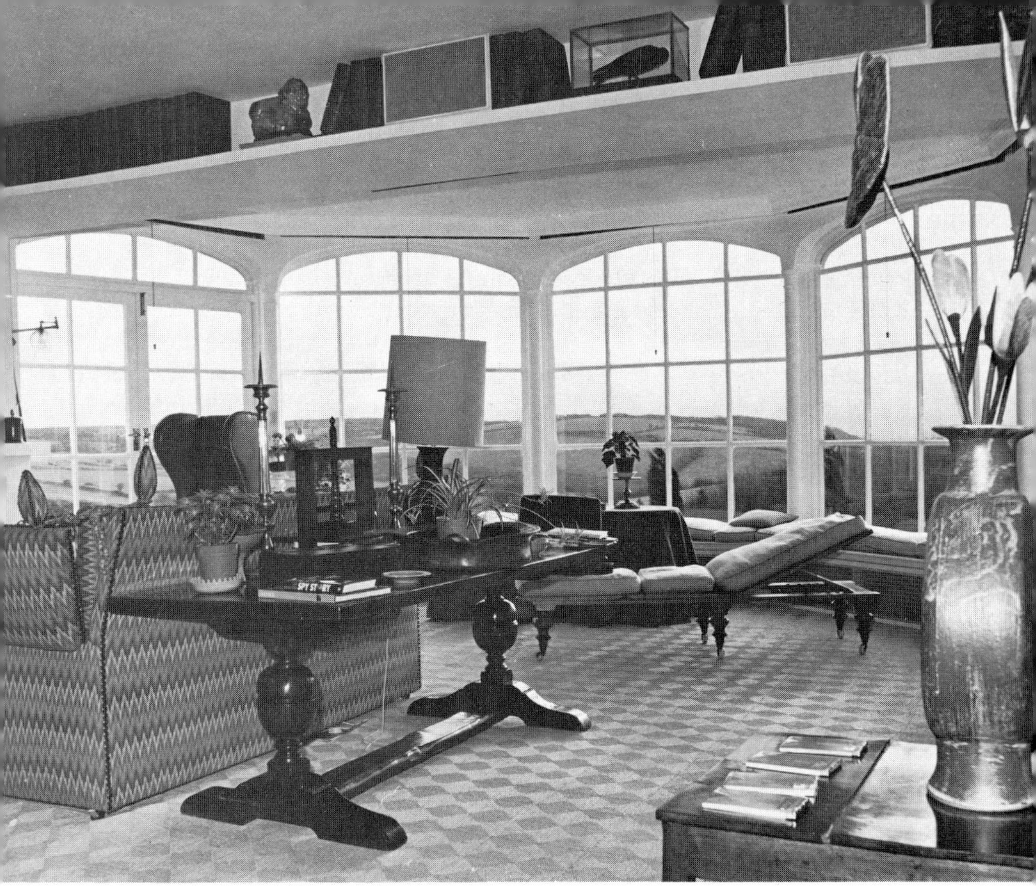

The library at Maidenwell.

gramme called *Quest for the Unicorn* in which she talked frankly about her condition. Viewers, like relations and close friends, were all impressed by her immense courage—not a hint of self-pity.

She died at her home on Bodmin Moor on a Sunday morning in October 1982, aged 44.

Fellow Bossiney author Sarah Foot, writing her obituary in *The Western Morning News,* said, 'She was the most courageous person I have ever known and she showed the full strength of her bravery right until her death when, as her husband Robin told me, "She orchestrated everything right until the end."

'Eight years ago I went to help Marika when her secretary was ill. It was then that I realised what pressure she worked under, rising at 4 a.m. so she could get in a few hours hard work before others were up and about and the telephone started ringing.

'She was always delighted to be planning large parties, and almost every week-end the house was full of guests.

'Sometimes when she felt low she would shut herself in the kitchen and cook. She always said she found it therapeutic.

'Even then it occurred to me that anyone living under such pressure would burn themselves out. It was awe-inspiring and slightly frightening to see the way she threw herself into life, performing every task with equal enthusiasm and energy. She was fanatic about never letting people down and meeting deadlines . . .

'A couple of weeks before Marika died I went to see her with my parents. She was in bed and likely to be there until the end. We knew this, and so did she, and yet her bedroom was not at all a sick room. Though her voice had changed and her face was puffy from drugs, she still looked pretty and composed and lively, wanting to know all the news.

'As my father told her the story of my brother who was involved in an exciting new project she suddenly lifted her pathetic thin arms above her head, and smiling said, "Isn't life wonderful?"

'All her life Marika was such a practical and efficient person, and had this mythical love affair with unicorns. She was always convinced she would see one, perhaps in her water garden, perhaps on the moor near her house.

'It was a strange and unexpected side to her character. But now I feel sure that Marika has found her Unicorn.'

Incredibly—and yet characteristically—Marika's cookery column appeared in *The Sunday Telegraph* the very day she died.

Doctor A. L. Rowse, writing also in *The Western Morning News,* reflected: 'With Marika Hanbury Tenison's death a light has gone out from Cornwall. Hers was a remarkable personality, gifted, gay, above all generous.

'A newcomer from Sweden to English life, she made a distinguished contribution to our country by her books and writing, not only in the field where she was an expert, the art and practice of cookery, setting us standards of good food. There were also her children's books, and her appreciation of travel and primitive peoples, a subject on which her talented husband is a master, and where she gave him valuable support.

'She loved Cornwall and the beautiful home she and her husband created on Bodmin Moor—which they made home for so many people from all countries. Their hospitality there was famous, as was the public-spirited work for Cornwall, with whose interests they identified themselves.'

We, at Bossiney, are especially proud of the fact that she contributed a chapter for our *Cornish Year Book* on Cornish Cooking.

Knowing that she was ill, and wondering whether she would still be interested in Bossiney after the disasters of *Meal*, I had doubts about the wisdom of approaching her.

But her response was warm and positive. 'I've got this Cancer thing,' she said in a telephone call, 'but I am intending to continue as if nothing is wrong. When's my deadline?'

Maidenwell, the home Marika and her husband created on Bodmin Moor. 'She had this mythical love affair with unicorns.'

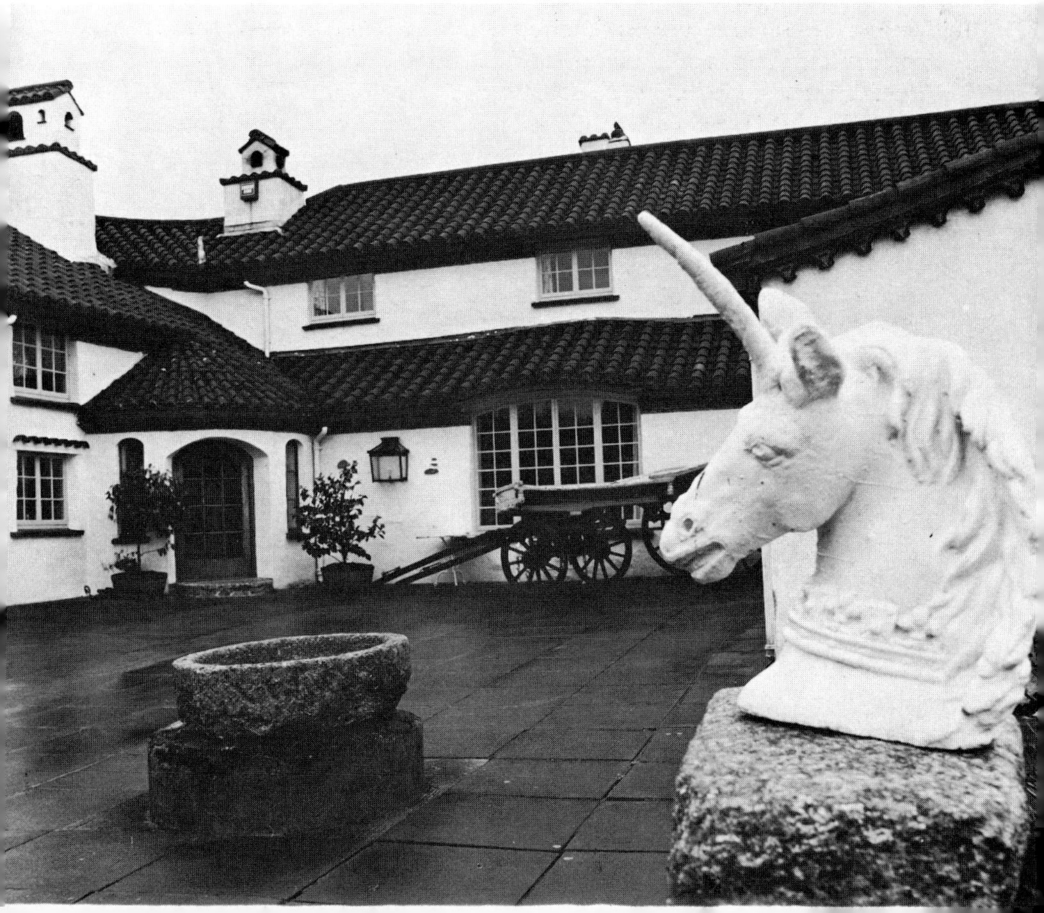

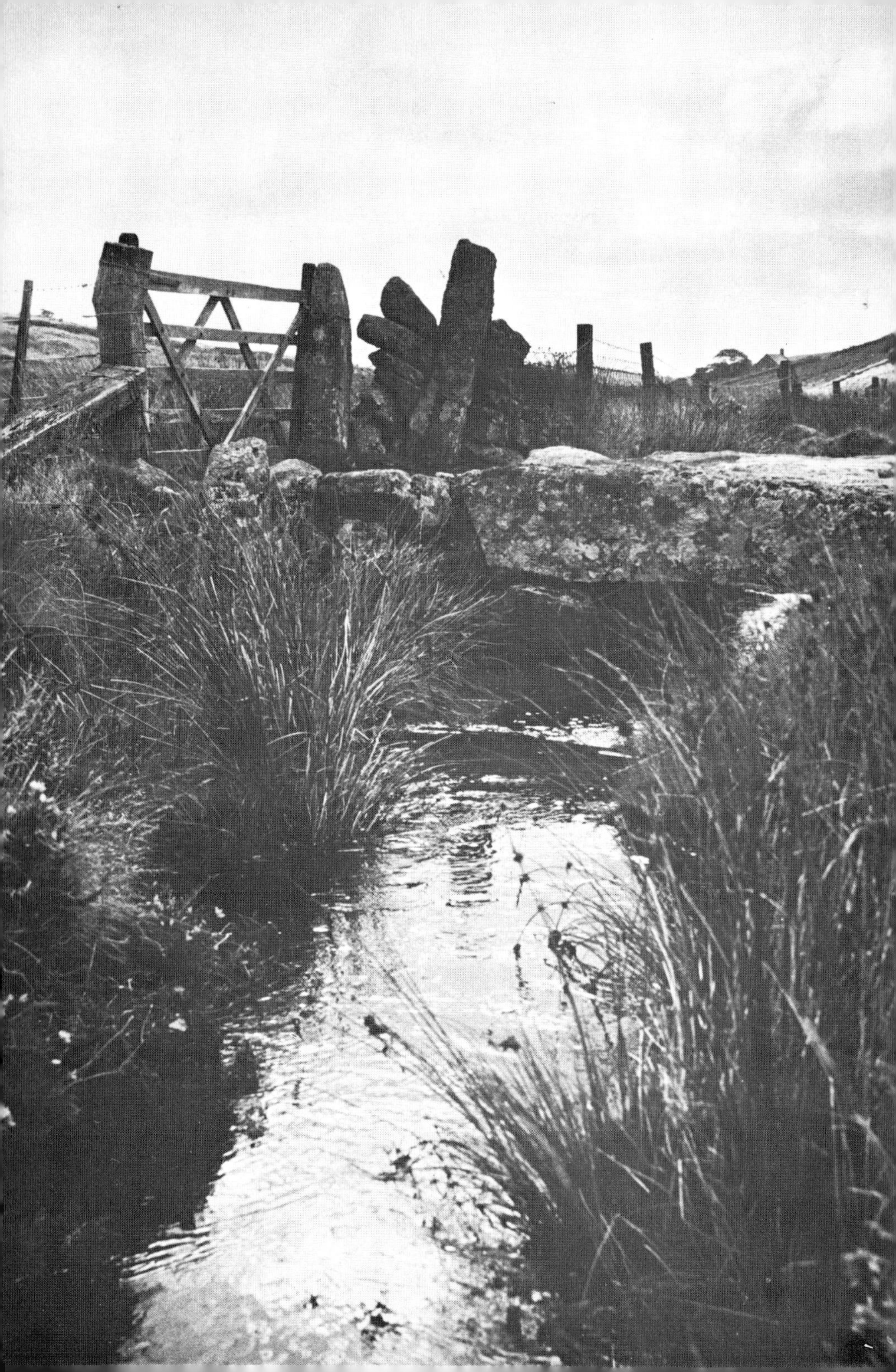

Thankfully she lived to see its appearance, and was so delighted with her complimentary copies that she ordered a parcel of books as 'Christmas presents'.

Alas she did not see Christmas, but we were all pleased that she liked the finished product, and I like to think of her last paragraph in that chapter as vintage Hanbury Tenison:

'The fame of the Cornish pasty spread throughout the world. One of the nicest things that has ever happened to me was arriving in a remote mining area in South America, in the middle of nowhere, and being greeted not just in my own language but in a broad dialect by a true 'Cousin Jack' working there, an ex-patriot from Cornwall. "Just in time for crib," he said, and led us into a rough wooden shack where he gave us thick black tea and pasties, fried rather than baked and extremely spicy, but nevertheless totally similar in shape and size to those we have at home. "If you are Cornish" said the bearded elderly miner, "you have to have your pasty a day to keep you going." '

Marika came to live on Bodmin Moor in 1960:
'. . . how fortunate I am to live here.'

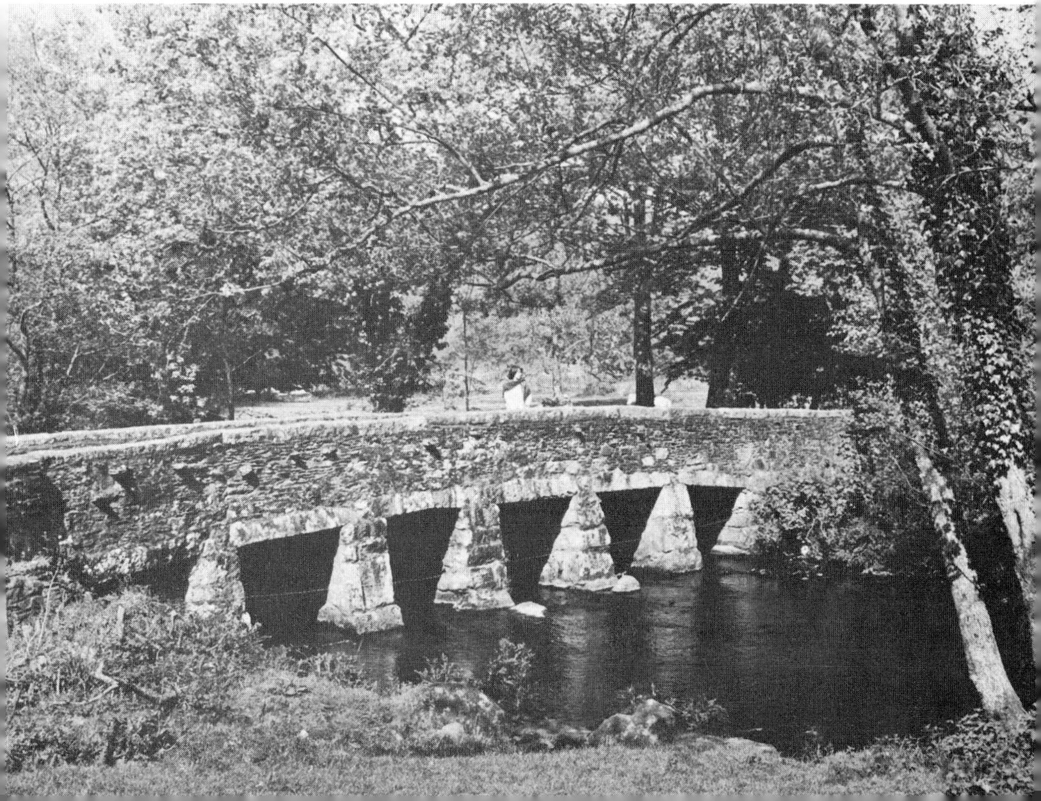

Rowena Cade
The Minack Theatre

The coastline of Cornwall is punctuated with beautiful beaches. My special favourite is Pedn-Vounder down in Penwith. It is a magical place. Porthcurno Bay, too, is lovely. It was used for the closing sequences of the first TV series *Poldark*, based on the brilliant best selling novels of Winston Graham.

On top of one rugged Porthcurno cliff, nearly 300 miles from the West End of London, you will incredibly meet a theatre box office, admittedly a grey concrete construction, but a box office all the same.

Penwith has this talent of springing surprises—some man-made others designed by Nature or accident. The Minack is neither. Standing here you may well ask: 'Did some Greeks, long ago, discover this corner of Penwith and resolve to build something to remind them of their cultural heritage?'

The idea is appealing, but the answer is 'No'. The facts are more modern, more down to earth. Quite simply, the Minack is the triumph *and* memorial of one remarkable lady: Miss Rowena Cade.

Like thousands of other Cornish people, I owe a considerable something to Miss Cade. Eighteen months in Bristol, for National Service, awakened in me a love of live theatre, and on coming back to Cornwall the interest was sustained by ten summers of visiting and watching plays at the Minack. On a few occasions, I even helped out at the box office. So the theatre and its creator have very special places in my Penwith memories.

Apart from meeting her dozens of times at the theatre, she also gave me two interviews for magazine features. Looking back I don't think I did a very good job of them, but, in fact, she was not the easiest of interviewees. Her modesty was an impediment—that was my experience anyway—and I sensed that she preferred to let the Minack speak for itself.

Dorothy Rowena Cade, trowel in hand, working on some seats at the Minack in 1960. King Charles spaniels were her companions for many years.

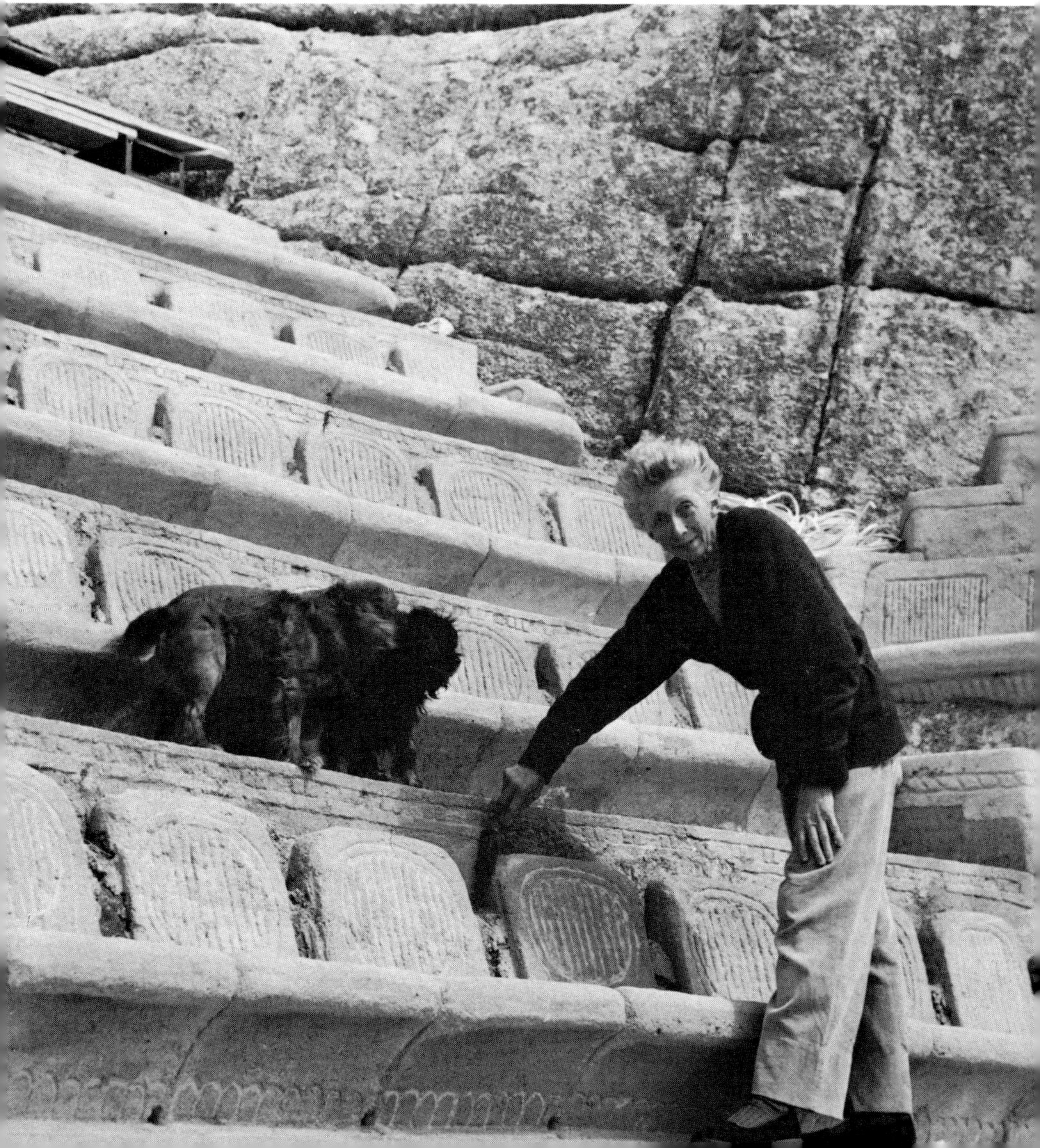

The Minack is—or was—a theatre in a private garden. But to begin at the beginning we must go to a wooded dell at Crean, a valley some three miles away near St Buryan.

There, by a stream, in August 1929 a group of local theatrical enthusiasts performed *A Midsummers Night's Dream* supported by the Penzance Orchestra, conducted by Walter Barnes. Shakespeare himself could not have imagined a more beautiful setting.

Such was the success of the occasion that Rowena Cade, who lived in a spacious house just off the Porthcurno-St Levan road, decided to explore the theatrical possibilities of her extensive Minack cliff gardens. In 1930 there was a steep slope of cliff. Together with her gardener Bill Rawlings and another Cornishman, Charles Angove,

The Minack Theatre: 'Her sense of theatre, her feel for drama and the marvellous application of her skills of craftsmanship and design have enriched the lives of thousands . . .'

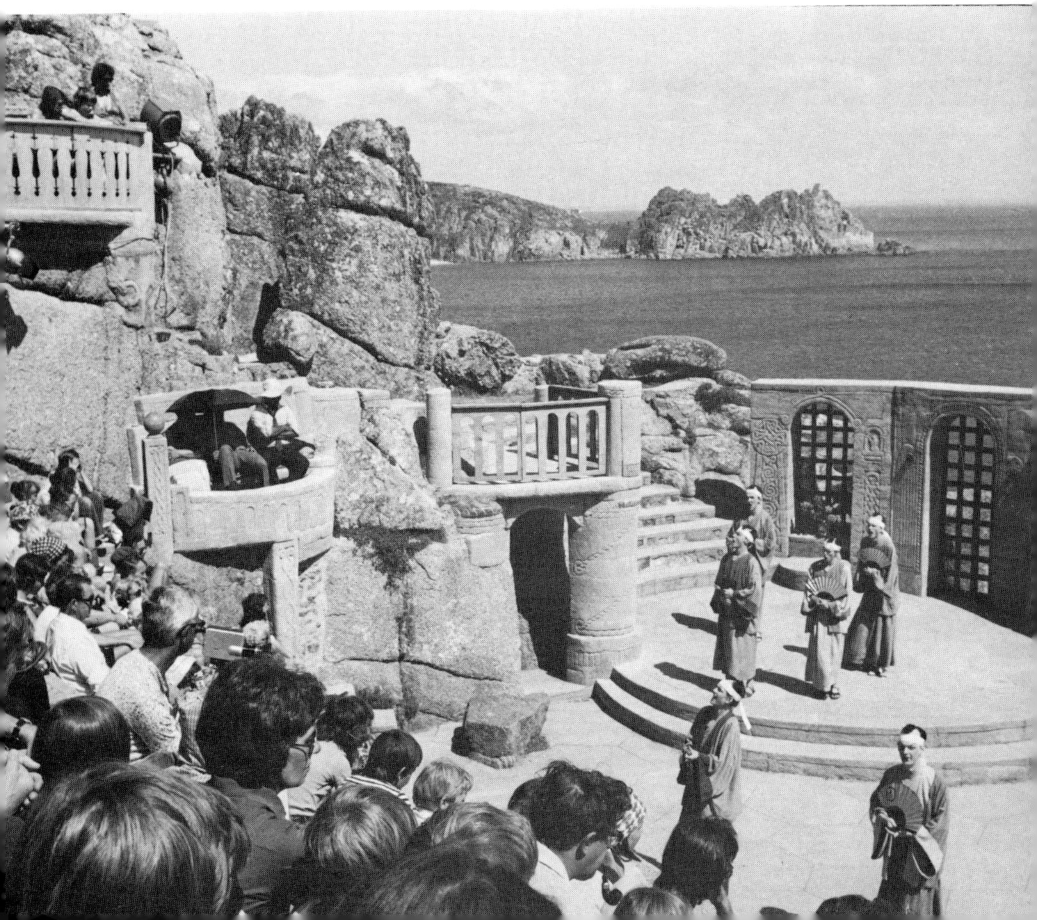

Miss Cade started work after Christmas in 1932 and by that August they had built an open-air theatre of a sort: the terrace turfed and with levels for seating. In Rowena Cade's own words: 'We did a rough-and-ready job for what we thought would be a week's acting. So you can call the Minack Theatre a do-it-yourself job!' Initially the stage ran straight over the cliff. Gradually, though, walling began to take shape and over the years, under Rowena Cade's leadership and through her vision, the Minack has grown into a unique theatre experience, giving pleasure to thousands of threatre-goers.

The theatre takes its name from the gigantic rock Minack which sprawls dramatically beneath. Eight productions were staged at the Minack before Hitler's war brought matters to a halt. In 1944 a film company came here to make *Love Story*, featuring Stewart Grainger and Margaret Lockwood. Live theatre was resumed in 1949 when the Penzance Girls' Grammar School presented *The Trojan Woman*, and two summers later Nora Ratcliff's *Tristan of Cornwall* began a sequence of annual productions which has grown into a full summer season.

The bulk of the work in building and shaping of the Minack Theatre has been done by Miss Cade and her faithful gardener Billy Rawlings; and after Billy's death this remarkable lady went on creating and improving.

Most of the permanent features of the theatre are of concrete, painstakingly carved with Cornish crosses and Celtic designs. Local people have often seen the flickering light of a torch there in the evening as Miss Cade finished off a particular piece before the concrete hardened.

In the celebrated 'gulley' part of the auditorium the back of each seat carries one of the many titles of plays performed there since 1932 with the appropriate date.

For years the tall distinguished figure of Rowena Cade, accompanied by her small group of King Charles Spaniels—she bred them—could frequently be seen carrying a weighty bag of sand or shouldering a piece of driftwood climbing the rugged path from Porthcurno beach: items that were often incorporated into the building of her theatre.

Richard Angove, a friend and neighbour for more than half a century, recalls: 'Miss Cade enjoyed nothing better than long walks on the familiar cliff paths which stretch out on both sides from her clifftop home. On stormy winter days, when the white-capped Atlantic rollers driven before hurricane-force winds climbed high around the Minack, she could be seen striding into the gale with her little dogs, their fine fur ruffled by the wind as they foraged in the close windswept cover.'

Another man who knows the Minack well is Douglas Williams, the Cornish Bard, author, journalist, broadcaster, singer and actor. He admits the theatre, 'just like everything else in Cornwall, has changed with the years. I've managed to span the post-war years there by playing in the first production after the war, in 1949, in Euripides' *The Trojan Women* and in 1977 in the Edward German comic opera for Silver Jubilee year, *Merrie England*... probably as great a contrast as one can imagine!

'Then there were no dressing rooms in the "wings", no lighting schemes, no acres of concrete. Then there was that gracious green-turfed stage—fatal for ballet dancers on a damp evening!—the walk down the lane from the changing rooms in Miss Cade's bungalow before the start of the performance, and the long climb back again in costume at the final "curtain call". Today there is more order, more theatrical facilities and equipment, plenty of carparking space, a hard-surfaced stage . . . and more concrete.

'Yet it is always a powerful physical experience to work here, as well as the expected emotional one to remember. This is what an audience often fails to realise, that physically for the players it is so much harder work—so much larger than life—than the traditional theatre. And often colder, wetter and draughtier!

'In those days more than thirty years ago there was a greater sense of freedom, and I think the "magical" spirit of the Minack was more apparent, particularly on a summer's day. Today the real beauty of the Minack comes at night on a "midnight matinée" with a full moon overhead, the Lizard Light twinkling, the Mount's Bay calm, the lights of the fishing boats passing nearby.

'For whatever else changes at the Minack, that magnificent natural backcloth remains the dominant feature of any production. Whatever is going on down on that stage, there is always a host of diversions beyond the stage, and around about and above us.

'Perhaps the most vivid memory for me came during the first night of *Merrie England*, when the final half-hour imprinted the scenes for life. There were cracking crashes and rolls of thunder and great bursts of light... but no rain until we were on our way home.

'The vision of Herne the Hunter on the distant Minack rock became a thrilling and startling silhouette as the lightning flashed about. What actor could compete with this—what director could rival it? Yes, I think Nature will always be the Minack's prima donna.'

John Bryant, who produced ten West Cornwall Theatre Group productions at the Minack, was also a neighbour of Miss Cade's. 'In the last years, she kept my telephone number by her bedside in case she needed help. But she never rang: a very independent spirit.

'Dorothy Mary Rowena Cade, that was her full name, came from Derbyshire. She and her family came to Cornwall in the 1920s with chauffeur and servants. They built North and South Minack House and later the "ruin" which was used for painting by her sister—Miss Cade, in fact, spent her last years there in the "ruin".

'She was a direct descendant of Wright of Derby, he painted during the Industrial Revolution, a great man for light. She lived a rather monastic life in a single room for those last fifteen years. She preferred it that way with her five or six King Charles spaniels; she was more than a builder of this theatre, she was an authority on the breed.

'She loved driving cars at speed. I can still see her face lighting up as she recalled the excitement. She was also religious, and regularly attended St Levan Church. She went through a phase of "High Church" but later came back to wanting a very simple service.

'Her physical efforts were tremendous, often starting her day at seven in the morning. She'd carry eight to a dozen plastic bags of sand from the beach, and until about ten years ago she even hauled water and cement down to the theatre. She was quite an eccentric lady; knew a great deal about plays, especially Shakespeare's. A very well-read lady which was surprising because she seemed to be so busy, physically building the theatre. She would watch the companies, local companies, and the visiting ones, and from her observations she added. The growth of the Minack was very much a bat and ball game, a bouncing off of ideas between her and local theatre people.

'I once offered to help her with some work at the theatre, but I wasn't quick enough for her. She said, at one point, "I thought you had gone home!" She had this immense energy. I can remember her painting the outside of her two houses when she was way into her seventies.

'The fact is she preferred working alone in her quiet purposeful way. I think she only enjoyed working with one person, and that was her gardener Billy, when she could have a wonderful swearing match when something went wrong.'

Another, who knew Miss Cade well is Geoff Helmore, a man who has played and directed at the Minack for more than a quarter of a century. 'I first met Miss Cade in 1957,' he recalled. 'One thing that stands out in my memory was attending a Minack Theatre Sub-Committee meeting and spending what seemed hours deciding on publicity, on how many posters, large and small, and handbills we should print.

'Then at the next meeting, she said, "I didn't like what we'd arranged; so I ordered so many of this size and that . . ." roughly doubling what we had agreed. Then, the following year, we'd go through precisely the same performance! She was wonderfully eccentric, in a quite delightful way. She had a natural dignity. She needed support, especially in the early days, and would say quite genuinely: "I really would like your advice."

'But she could be very autocratic. There was a Greek play which had recently been translated, and because we thought it would be popular we asked if we could perform it at the Minack. But her reaction was definite: "No I don't want *that* play in my theatre!" Hers was the final decision.

'I have one special memory of her, a very personal one. My late wife and I had met through the Minack, and we were only able to manage a weekend honeymoon locally, and, though it was winter, sentimentally we went down to the Minack that weekend. It was a very stormy day, heavy rain and tremendous seas running. But we were so happy we didn't care. We even went on stage and said a few lines, when suddenly to our astonishment Rowena Cade appeared from behind some rocks and asked "What are you doing here?" After we told her, we asked the same question, "What are *you* doing here?"

"Well," she said, "if the rain clears, I might make a bit of cement."

'She watched the players there with a critical eye. Without question, she had a great knowledge of the theatre, and she knew what she liked, and *why* she liked it. The plays she liked were the classics, especially Shakespeare.

'The great accolade for visiting companies was on the Thursday evening of their week, when Miss Cade would leave a tray of peaches in the dressing room with a note saying, "I enjoyed your play." But, one company, one year, put a lavatory on the stage as part of the play's setting. Miss Cade didn't approve and they didn't get any peaches.'

Her death, at the age of 89, in March 1983, marked the end of a Penwith era. Lawrence Shrove, the Minack's manager from 1968 to 1981, writing an appreciation of this amazing lady in *The Western Morning News* recalled:

'Rowena Cade had two favourite viewpoints of the Minack Theatre. One was the terrace, high above the theatre, where she sat in a tipped up wheelbarrow. The other was a perch on the gully wall, to which she walked sure-footed as a cat, along a narrow ledge, white hair blowing in the wind, dressed in baggy sweater and narrow black trousers, gym shoes gripping the rock.

'Always courteous nevertheless she found ways of conveying her

'. . . that magnificent natural backcloth remains the dominant feature of any production.'

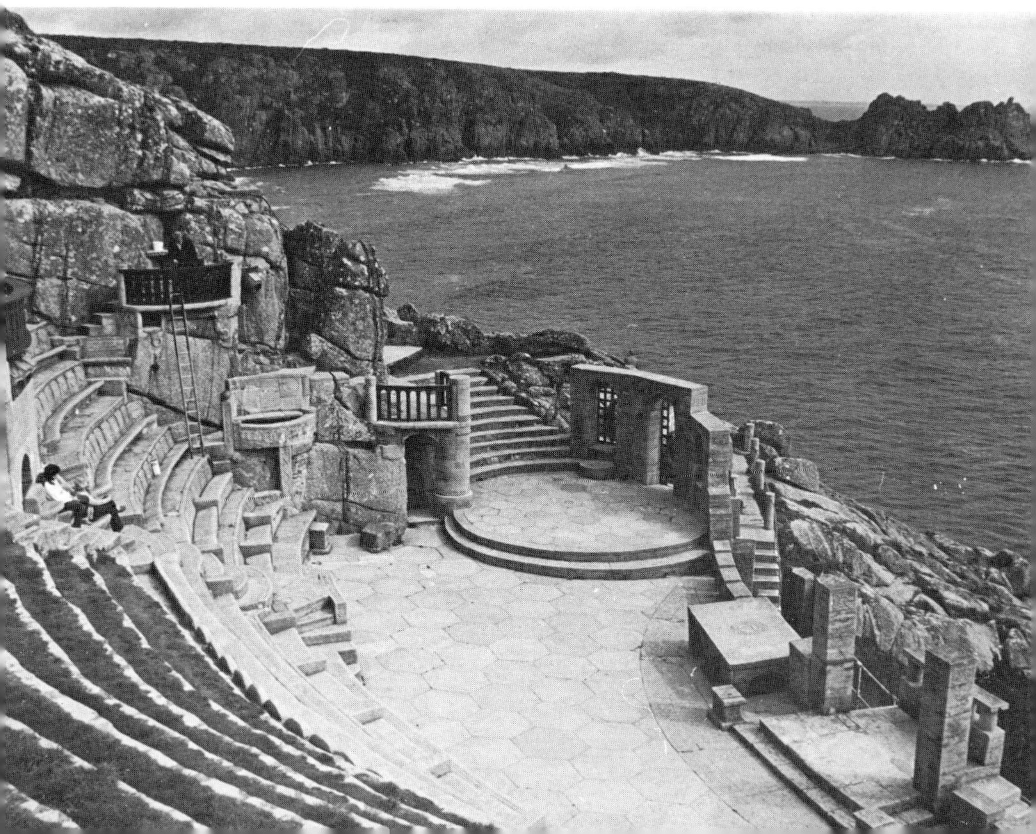

views on a production: she invariably saw it through once insisting on paying for a seat and programme but the return visits were the accolade! In later years she became deaf but her deafness was highly selective; she never heard anything she deemed it better to ignore!

'She leaves behind her a theatre which is unique, spectacular and timeless. That must be her memorial. Companies, though, never forget the joy of seeing her again at the start of a tour at The Minack or the sadness of bidding her farewell. It is a measure of her indestructable nature that no one can quite believe that it is farewell forever.'

At a Memorial Service of Thanksgiving held at the Minack on Sunday 1 May 1984, an address was given by the Bishop of Truro, the Right Reverend Peter Mumford. I wrote to the Bishop asking if I may quote him inside these pages.

In his reply the Bishop wrote: 'I am very honoured to contribute my little meditation about Rowena Cade, and I had very full notes in my files which I've been able to reproduce for you just as the little sermon was preached. I did not know Miss Cade well, though I had met her once, and therefore these were rather more reflections about her contribution than a description or tribute . . .'

Here is what the Bishop, a Vice President of the theatre, said at the service:

'This is not so much an "Address"; more a meditation necessarily brief and fragmentary, as was my acquaintance with the great Miss Cade. We are meeting in the Easter season; Christian minds go to that event which made possible the continuing presence in his world of the Creator, who took human form. By his bursting from the tomb of defeat and oblivion Christ our Lord gave assurance and hope to a world forlorn. As we say in a prayer of today, "He gave us grace and opened the gate of Glory."

'The Easter truth and the events which led up to it, and those which followed, are not only the most vital of moments in history; they also form the central drama of human life. They express in vivid actuality that which is always true: that hope is more inspiring than despair, laughter more humanising than anger, and love the ultimate conqueror of hate.

'All theatre is a focus of the human condition: it compresses into a single hour what is a lifetime or a whole millennium of experience; it renders significant and memorable a trivial happening, a passing idea that witnesses to the universal verities.

'Because of this compression all drama is, at its profoundest level, religious. The highlighting of human experience and the ennobling of human sentiment are not far removed from the unfolding of the Divine purpose through the unique, miraculous coming, dying and rising of the Saviour God.

'In Rowena Cade we have seen one who saw far and achieved much. Her sense of theatre, her feel for drama and the marvellous application of her skills of craftsmanship and design have enriched the lives of thousands and pointed us to eternal truths.

'May the Christ who—in her own words read just now *(The Robin)*—"entered our instant pain" bring her and us to "the eventual light".

Denys Val Baker
Penwith

Denys Val Baker lived in various parts of Cornwall, but I felt his heart was always in Penwith.

He was Welsh by descent, but deeply Cornish in his writing and essentially Celtic in his response to the Cornish landscape, particularly that area west of Hayle.

He, more than any other writer, alive or dead, tried to get to the root of Cornwall's magnetism for the creative spirit. In *Britain's Art Colony by the Sea*, published in 1959—one of my favourite Cornish books—he wrote:

'The explanation is not a simple one. It is a mixture of material and mystical, facts and fantasies, all equally important. The climate, the brilliant light, the almost Mediterranean blue of the sea, the fascinating formations of rocks and cliffs, hills and valleys, sand and pebble shores—these are some of the more obvious attractions. So, too, is the comparative freedom and easiness of life in a small but cosmopolitan town such as St Ives, as compared to most of the provincial towns and industrial areas; the congenial atmosphere of working and living among large groups of fellow artists; the facilities of numerous art galleries and show-rooms, several art societies, clubs and other meeting places; and last but by no means least, a sympathetic population and press, conditioned by several decades of growing up alongside the art colony, so that what might seem an oddity if dumped in some other part of Britain has come to be taken for granted in Cornwall.

'This is an important point, but it does not provide a final answer

Denys Val Baker (right): '. . . undoubtedly did more than any other man or woman of his time to encourage writing in Cornwall.'

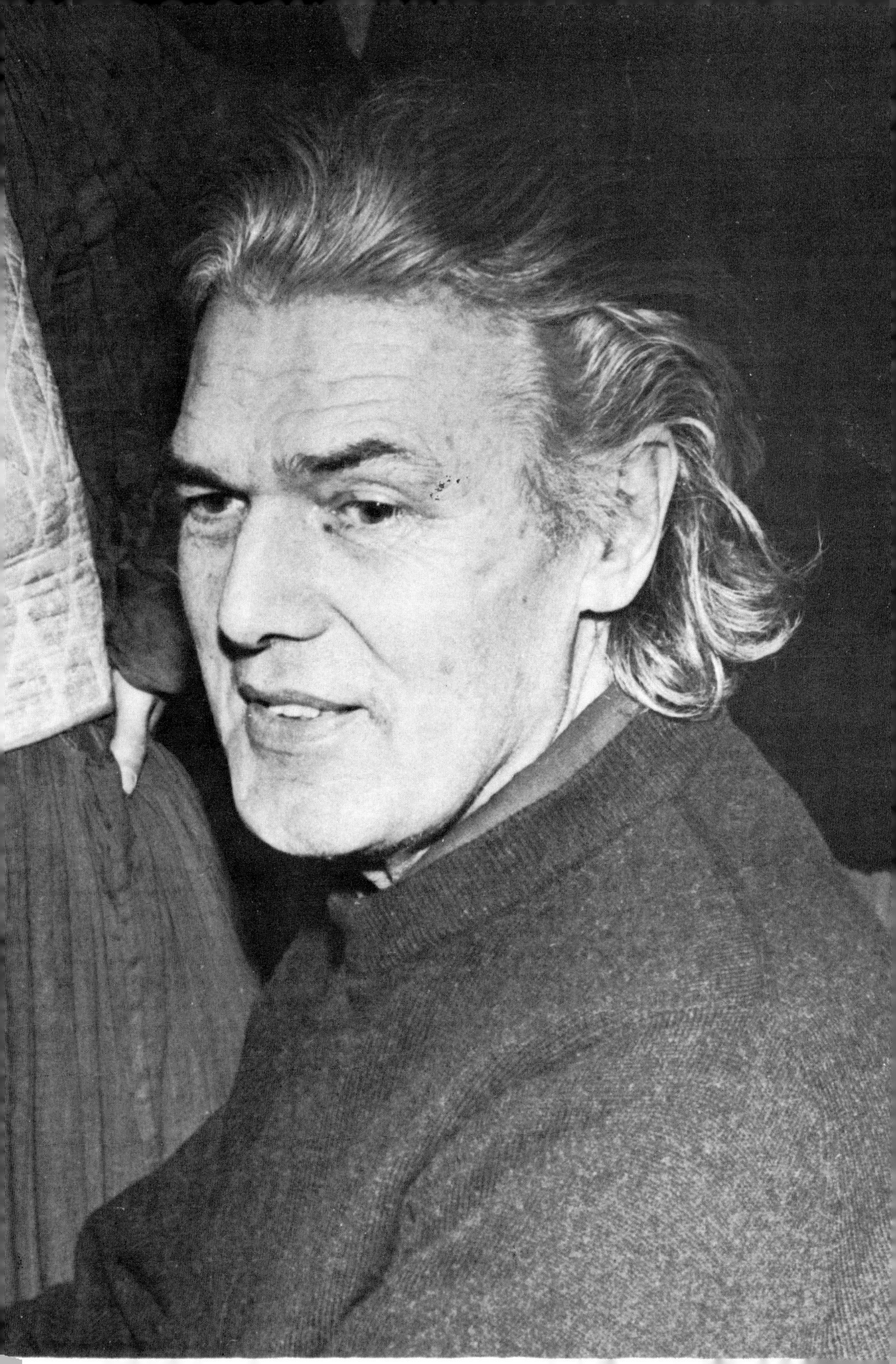

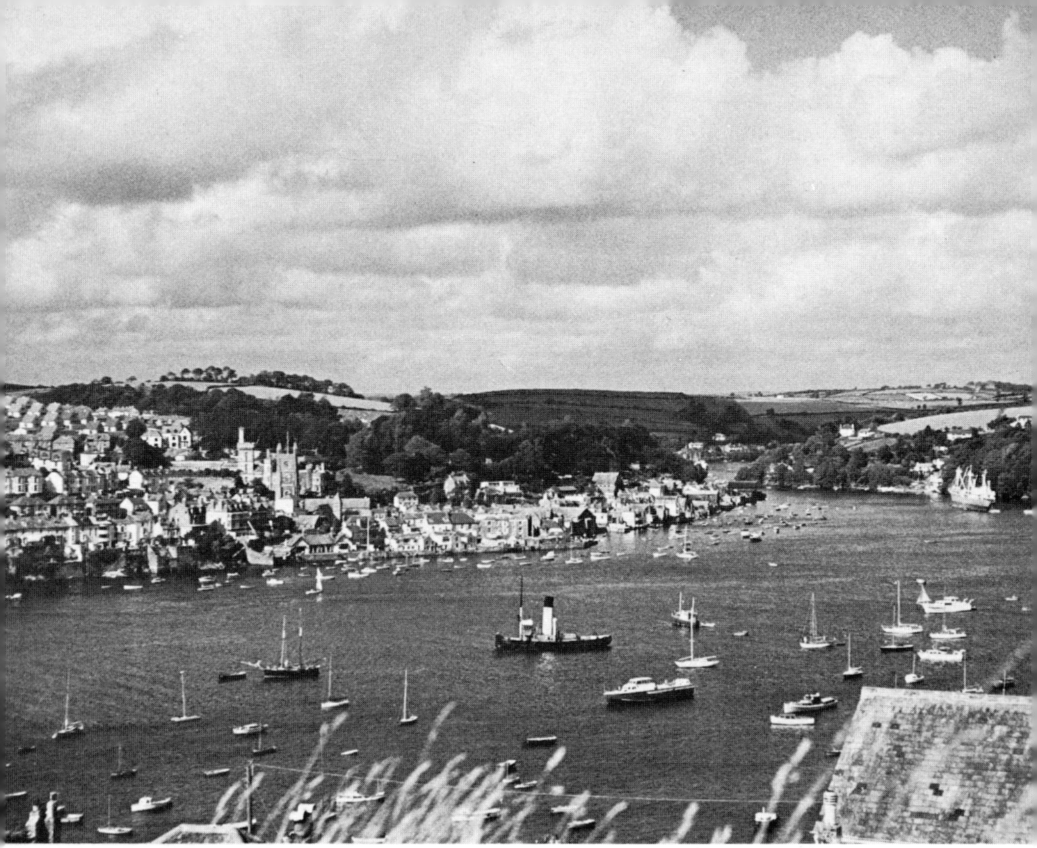

Denys must have sailed this stretch of river at Fowey many times in his boat *Sanu* when the family lived upriver on the banks of the Fowey.

to the question, it does not elucidate the real explanation which remains hidden somewhere in Cornwall itself. Perhaps it is some sort of force, a magnetic force (for Cornwall draws artists like a magnet pulling with some underlying hidden strength which cannot be resisted). So many perceptive writers and artists of all kinds have recorded their experience of this hidden force, this strange, brooding, compelling quality, and its influence and inspiration have been apparent in so many books as well as paintings, that the mystery must be accepted even if it cannot be adequately explained in words.'

Personally, I look back on the life of Denys Val Baker with particular gratitude. He not only gave me some wonderful writing opportunities for *The Cornish Review*—he also encouraged me to venture into publishing, and it was, in fact, Denys, over dinner at Bossiney House, who said, 'Your company can have only one name: Bossiney Books. It's so right.' He was rarely dogmatic, but he was absolutely certain this should be our name.

Whereas some wise friends warned me the age of the cottage publisher was over, and only the heavy artillery with London offices and nationwide distribution could survive in modern publishing, Denys was sure there was still a place for the small regional publisher, and he was kind enough to say to someone, 'Michael Williams is the ideal man to publish Westcountry authors.' Outside and beyond all this, Denys made a positive contribution to the Bossiney cause by contributing a fine chapter to one of our early titles: *My Cornwall* in which a star-studded team of authors wrote a chapter each: authors like the du Maurier sisters, Daphne and Angela, Colin Wilson, Derek Tangye and Ronald Duncan among others. Denys, then enjoying sailing and literary success with his boat *Sanu*, wrote on Cornwall seen from the sea.

Here is how he ended that chapter. To me, it's vintage Val Baker.

'Well quite often aboard *Sanu*, we have indeed been "out there" in some such stormy seas—probably in fact, not at all as far "out there" as we would have liked, for in bad weather the more sea room the better. At such times the close proximity of all those rugged cliffs, those craggy rocks, those evil looking underwater obstructions—is neither romantic nor mysterious or edifying in any way—they are simply quite terrifying. Under such conditions, with white crested waves cascading high in the air as they break on distant rocks—with great rollers roaring up some not distant enough white sandy beach—with spray often clouding the very top of cliffs—one would give almost anything in the world to be a thousand miles away from the cursed Cornish coastline!

'But then, a day later, the scene has changed again. The sun shines, the sea sparkles, the boat glides gently along, on yet another fascinating pilgrimage along one of the most intricate and most mysterious, and the most beautiful coastlines in the whole wide world. And if, as dusk falls, one is inclined to remember Mrs Manning Sanders' wise words—"It is then the place becomes haunted, a giant heaves grey limbs from his granite bed, a witch sits in that stone chair on the cliff"—well, isn't that really what makes Cornwall so rare and wonderful and magical a place?'

Back in 1969, Denys asked me to review his latest book *Adven-*

tures Before Fifty in *The Cornish Review*. Looking back, I now realise this was quite a compliment. He could have asked many more distinguished contributors to do the job, and characteristically said, 'You must only say you like it if you really mean it.' Re-reading that review recently was an odd experience, like meeting another person who shares your name.

Here is what I wrote:

'Gillian Tindall, who writes for *The Guardian*, hates the thought of being photographed in a cheerful mood when she is writing on a serious subject. There is also a theory that men, who have something worthwhile to say, must look forbidding, rather like a character carrying a warning notice: "Prepare to meet thy doom."

'I have a suspicion too that this grim approach stretches as far as the reviewers and their columns. So many critics clearly loathe read-

'I had long ago deserted London for . . . Cornish cliffs and carns and moors . . . and the booming echoes of the restless seas.' Carn Barges in West Penwith.

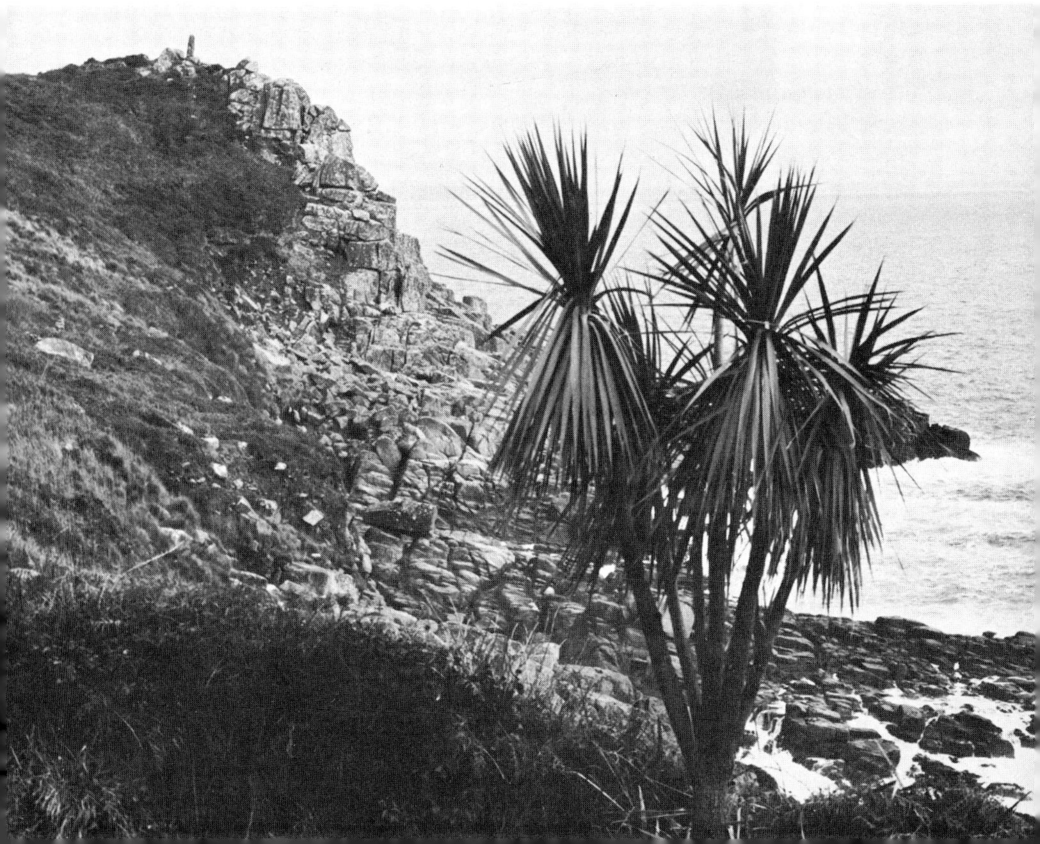

ing, and as for the quality of readability, they have turned it into a sin larger than lust or gluttony. In saying I found Denys Val Baker's latest book (and his biggest, roughly 160,000 words) both entertaining and readable, I shall probably be accused of giving it the kiss of death. However, I take that risk in venturing a prediction: no more readable, more entertaining book will come out of Cornwall this year. Though there is no need to equate a book and a toothpaste ad., why should a reviewer hesitate to use adjectives like readable and entertaining? Is not the author's objective to make the reader move from one sentence to the next—and to turn the page?

'Those of us who know Denys Val Baker's work, have met some of the incidents in *Adventures Before Fifty* on previous occasions, but this saga of misadventure covers a large slice of his life, giving a greater sense of continuity, revealing perhaps a deeper, more reflective assessment of people and situations. His views on St Ives' sad decline, for example, are interesting and perceptive. "Gone is the pretty and unspoiled fishing port that once existed—in its place, at least every summer, a noisy, brassy, over-crowded conglomeration of cafés and gift stores and fish and chip shops and everywhere the brightly painted bed and breakfast signs. It is probably nobody's fault but the damage is done: everywhere the values appear to be increasingly those of money and materials. In the most unlikely places ordinary, quite pleasant cottage fronts are suddenly converted into shop windows—full of Birmingham brassware, East End knicknacks, Hong Kong toys . . . It is like a vicious circle, or rather spiral—the end of which can dimly and dismally be foreseen." St Ives, he believes, is "in danger of becoming a sick town".

'And recalling the collapse of the first *Cornish Review*, he exposes the truth that, as a race, we Cornish are parochial: ". . . Cornwall is more of a continent than a county: that is, it is not so important that you are in Cornwall, what matters—drastically, irrevocably—is what part of Cornwall you come from."

'Yet his love of Cornwall is deep and lasting. On the very opening pages he explains why "it seemed perfectly natural to me that we should settle in Cornwall . . . I had long ago deserted the literary world of London for the wilder and more exciting setting of Cornish cliffs and carns and moors, and everywhere the booming echoes of the restless sea—I had for a long time been conscious of being drawn westwards to this strange and somehow primitive and mysterious land . . . I could not, in fact, imagine living anywhere else."

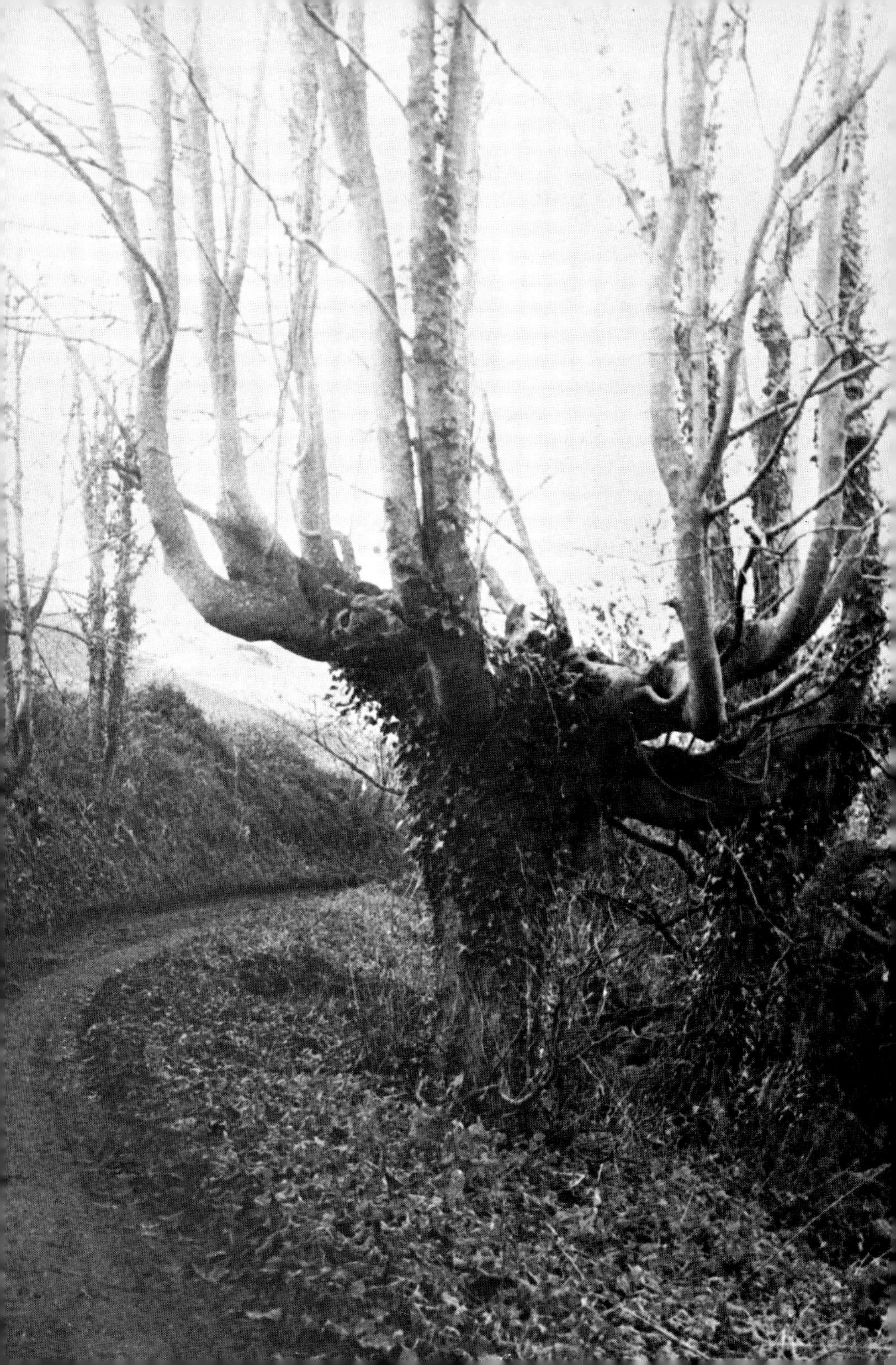

'. . . this strange brooding compelling quality . . . its influence and inspiration have been apparent in so many books as well as paintings . . .' Thus Denys Val Baker explained Cornwall's magnetism for the creative spirit.

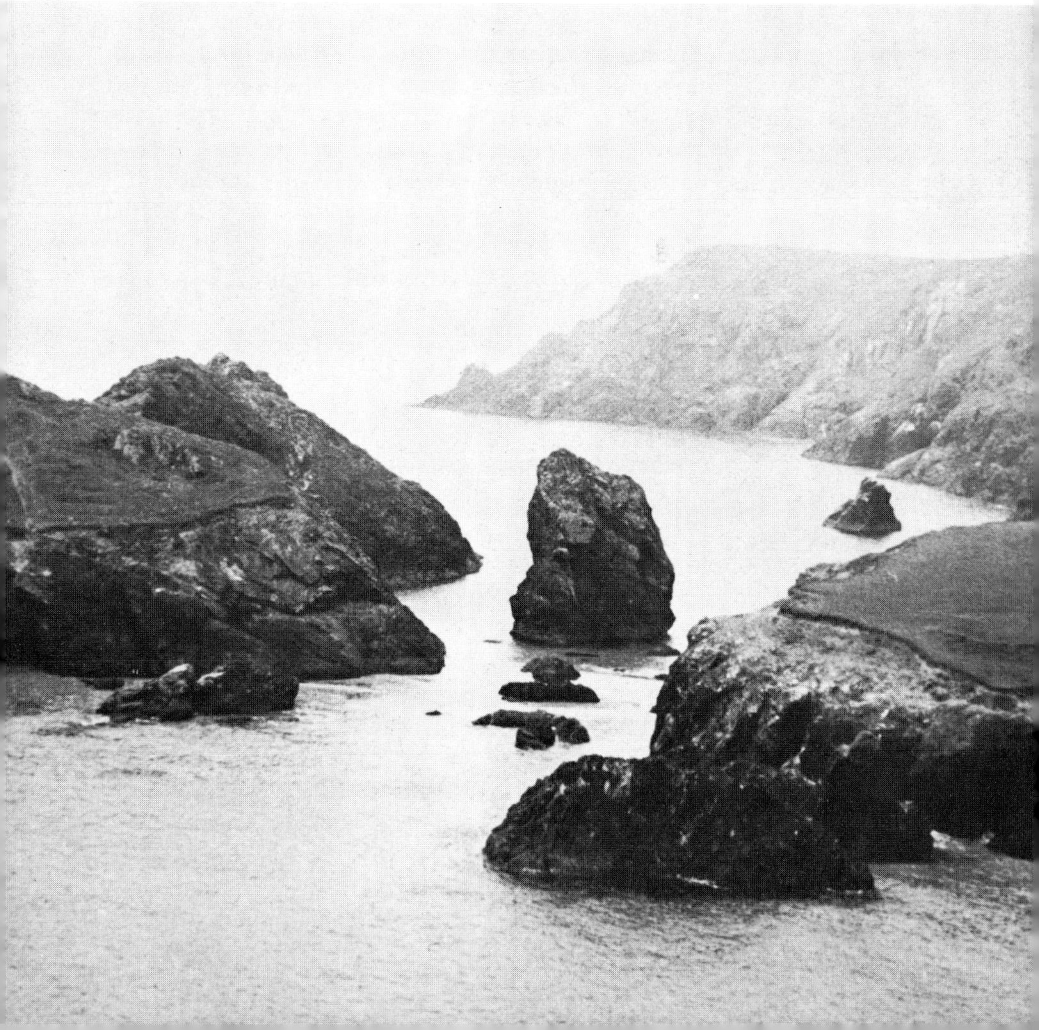

'Rightly, the blurb asks: "Has anyone else in the world crammed more misadventures into fifty years?"

'Hair-raising episodes pepper the pages. The Atlantic washing the kitchen floor at St Ives, plans for building a Utopia on a South Sea island, legal battle with *The People* newspaper, Ban the Bomb, un-Chichester-like sailing including shipwreck—these are only some of the bare bones of Life with the Val Bakers. Like Isadora's capital A for Art, the Val Bakers deserve a capital L for Life. Tom Salmon of the BBC has aptly described them as a family "destined to teeter forever on the edge of disaster" yet the word defeat somehow does not apply to them. And nearly always the wolf has been whining at their different doors. Their homes in Cornwall have been as different as the seasons of the year, only more numerous. A converted barn high up in the hills of Penwith, an isolated cottage at the Land's End, a Georgian house in Penzance, a seventeen-room vicarage (once occupied by Bernard Walke) at St Hilary, a castle on the north Cornish coast, a house on the beach at St Ives, and now The Old Sawmills up a creek off the River Fowey, near Golant—Iris Murdoch might have used any of them in a novel.

'A personality invariably emerges from any attempt at autobiography and from these 432 pages and fifty years, a several-sided author appears. Certainly a family man, certainly a campaigner against the conventional, a talented writer too—one who can make us chuckle.'

Curiously enough, fifteen years on, I basically stand by all I wrote about him on that occasion. Maybe the condemnation about reviewers was rather too general, too sweeping, and, in any case, I was referring to the men and women reviewing for the nationals.

Denys, I believed then, and still believe today, deserved better treatment at a national level. Ironically, when he died he had the lead obituary in *The Times*; while *The Guardian* gave him a generous half-column. How he would have benefitted from such coverage in his working lifetime. But that, as Miss Rantzen might have put it, *is* Life.

His lifestyle was essentially that of the freelance, and his struggle for independence—which meant supporting Jess and their growing family—fired Kenneth Allsop, the TV interviewer and book critic, to refer to his status as 'The Freedom of the stoker in Hell!'

The Guardian piece, written by a writer signing himself J.T. (J. C. Trewin perhaps) paid tribute to his autobiographical works.

'His sequence of autobiographies had a special quality—mercurial, spontaneous and charming, (he had a natural and gentle friendliness)—but they also revealed his cheerful courage in working for so long, and often against the odds, as a freelance writer firmly based in far Cornwall.'

Denys, though, was a considerable literary all-rounder: a short-story writer—one of the best Cornwall has produced—a novelist, autobiographer, editor of collections like *Stories of the Macabre*, editor and magazine publisher and essayist. And briefly he ventured into book publishing; he produced three titles under the imprint of The Cornish Library, but, like his *Review*, they did not get the backing they deserved.

His output was prodigious. He published twenty novels, 23 autobiographies, fifteen short story collections, six titles on general subjects, 43 edited collections of other writers' works and several hundred short stories. The short story was, in fact, his favourite form, and he deeply regretted not being able to give more time to this style of writing. Of the hundreds he created *The Woman & The Engine Driver* and *The Clay Pool* are especially fine examples. From 1972 until his death, he wrote for William Kimber and in those productive years he edited 23 anthologies of short stories by such writers as Winston Graham, Margaret Drabble, Daphne du Maurier, Edna O'Brien, Hammond Innes and Alan Sillitoe.

Denys undoubtedly did more than any other man or woman of his time to encourage writing in Cornwall. In 1949 he founded his *Cornish Review*. He saw the little magazine—in a broad sense—as an important shop window for aspiring talents in the Arts, and he practised what he preached. Denys, then living in a cottage on the edge of Trencrom Hill, with Jess, spent hour after hour sitting by their oil lamp sending out leaflets to lovers of Cornwall everywhere. The magazine received a warm reception, Howard Spring saying it was the duty of Cornish men and women to support the *Review*.

'It is fitting that this region should have a place for uttering its own voice, for it is a region of character, and idiosyncracy. Its people and climate, and their interaction, have produced something easily distinguished from anything that will be found elsewhere: and this is true despite the levelling consequences of our day. So long as that remains true there will be a reason for a magazine like this.'

But alas it died after only ten issues. Yet bravely—and typically

Denys—he resurrected it in the spring of 1966, this time with some support from the Arts Council and Cornwall County Council. Sadly, history repeated itself when both organisations withdrew their support—the second innings though was longer, the *Review* running from 1966 to the winter of 1974.

Both periods of publishing produced truly literary feasts. The early editions, now as rare as gold dust and genuine collectors' items, contained contributions by famous names like Bernard Leach, Jack Clemo, Charles Causley, Peter Lanyon, David St Thomas and Charles Marriott, then Art Critic of *The Times*. The second life of the magazine saw work from J. C. Trewin, D. M. Thomas, Noel Welch, Ida Procter and Frank Baker, and reproductions of paintings and drawings, coming from such celebrated painters as Margo Maeckleberghe, Jack Pender, Bryan Pearce, John Miller and Mary Jewells.

Writing in that sad final edition, the Editor reflected:

'Looking back as dispassionately as I can on the two separate "lives" of the *Cornish Review*, obviously the second series, with 27 issues has covered much wider ground but I am still inclined to think that the 1949-1952 numbers were possibly of a higher literary quality. Fortunately the difference is really only marginal—by and large the literary standard throughout, I feel confident is something of which Cornwall can be proud. For of course, in the last analysis it is Cornwall that inspired the *Cornish Review*—and I suppose in a sad sort of way, Cornwall that is responsible for its demise. The penultimate cause of the magazine's end is indeed a withdrawal of the SWAA grant, but also reluctance among the Cornish people themselves to give that really practical support to what was, after all, their own and only literary magazine. Why this should be so I really do not know: Cornish support for numerous local ventures—amateur dramatics, opera, music, etc.—is often very enthusiastic. Why then not for a literary magazine? Alas the *Cornish Review* bows out still unable to provide the answer to that question . . . perhaps some time in the future a new phoenix will rise and follow a happier flight path.'

This chapter would not be complete without reference to his wife Jess. A potter and considerable character in her own right, their marriage was a remarkable triumph, for anyone reading his autobiographical books will see and understand the strong part Jess played—indeed without Jess I doubt whether he would have become the writer he did. Moreover I have a hunch that Jess herself has a fine book or two inside her.

Denys and Jess Val Baker finally came back to Penwith—home some would say—in the early 1970s, to an old mill house at Tresidder near St Buryan. The move from Golant to Penwith is told

Nancledra: Granite is the very bones of West Penwith. 'Denys Val Baker lived in various parts of Cornwall, but I felt his heart was always in Penwith.'

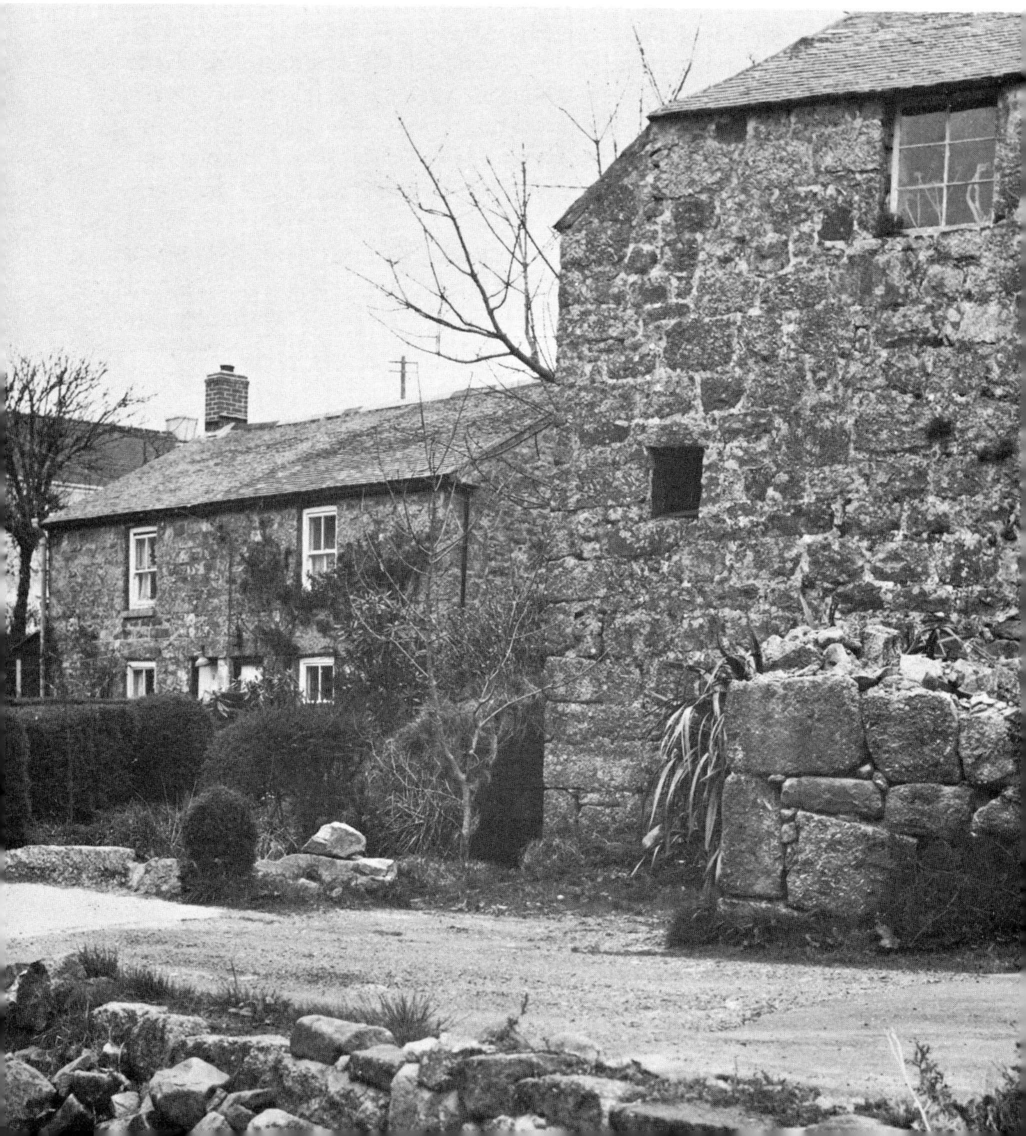

in his book *An Old Mill by the Stream*. From here he continued to write regularly until his death in 1984.

Denys was a Bohemian, a pacifist and a vegetarian, and, above all, a rebel against the Establishment, convention and bureaucracy. Nothing personified his Bohemian approach more vividly than his funeral held at the Truro crematorium. No vicar, no undertaker—the coffin was borne by his family—there were six children. No church music either: we were greeted by Sibelius's *Finlandia* and during the service his daughter Demelza and son Stephen sang his favourite song *I Want to be Free.*

Friends paid tribute to the man and the writer who was their friend. At the close there was Louis Armstrong's version of *Up a Lazy River* and an invitation to go back home to St Buryan. There were few black ties—most people were dressed as if they were going to a party or a day out shopping in Truro or Penzance—he would have liked that. No hint of hypocracy. It was, as someone said, rather like a Val Baker party—certainly not a funeral, more like 'a celebration'.

The most moving moments for me were when Kate Baker, widow of his old writer friend Frank, read *Epilogue*, written by Denys. It were as if the man was saying Farewell to us. In a way, he was, but in another way not, because, as the poet Charles Causley said, 'His work will live on.'

Here are the words which Kate Baker read:

Epilogue:

It was fun while it lasted,
Father Time.
Thanks for the interlude,
Of such love and such
laughter and life;
So rainbow hued,
For a time, Father Time,
for a time.

It was fun while it lasted,
Father Time.
Thanks for the chance,
Of childish games and

pretty names, and thanks
For a real romance,
For a time, Father Time,
for a time.

It was fun while it lasted,
Father Time.
Thanks for the glory,
Of sunshine and sea and
surf and sand, and thanks
For writing my story,
For a time, Father Time,
for a time.

Oh, yes, it was fun while it
lasted, Father Time.
So thanks for that stolen
hour,
Of precious life and kids
and wife, and thanks
Forever for that hour,
Of your time, Father Time,
of your time.

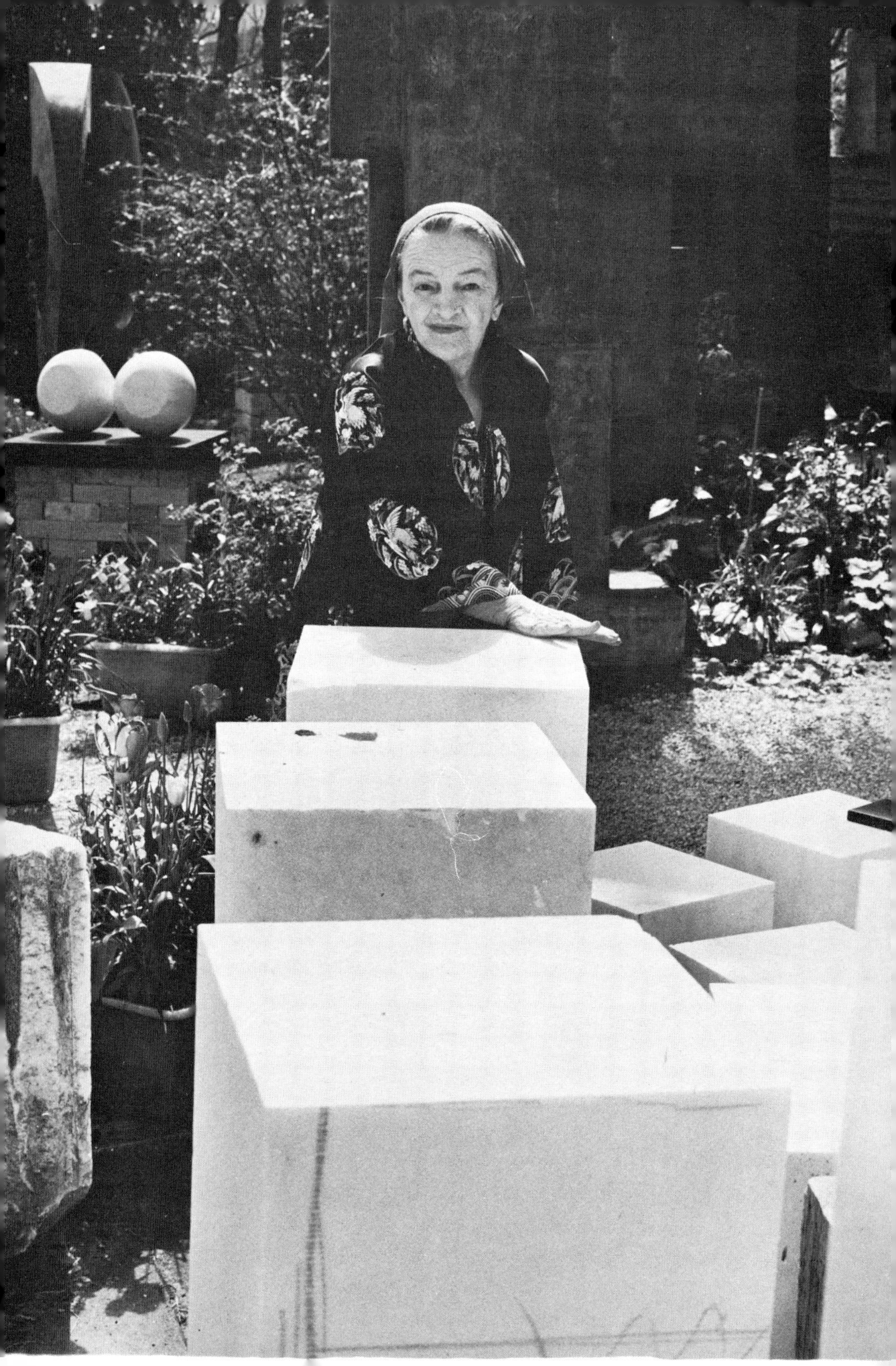

Dame Barbara Hepworth
St Ives

Though I was born just outside Penzance and lived and worked in the town for something like thirty years, I owe more to St Ives.

It was St Ives which opened my eyes.

For nearly thirty years, I saw next to nothing, but St Ives and especially its art galleries, changed all that and, in a strange way, for a time, became the window of my world. It was more than a matter of discovering that art is 'life enhancing'; deeper than the realisation that a painting can enrich life as can a poem or a piece of music. It was probably something to do with growing-up, something I never found inside any text book during what was laughingly called education.

Without coming face to face with the sculpture, the pottery and the paintings I would have grown into a very different and certainly a poorer character. The colours and the tones, the shapes and the rhythms of Penwith, I started seeing them for the first time.

Today St Ives is one of the West's most attractive holiday resorts, but two hundred years ago it was a busy port, shipping away Cornish copper and tin. Long trains of pack mules brought the minerals from as far afield as Pendeen and St Just, St Day and Redruth. One hundred years later the railway came, bringing the visitors.

St Ives manages various fine images: the harbour with boats bobbing about like bits of proverbial cork, or, when the tide is out, the ribbed sand revealed and the boats lying on their sides; the quaint cottages, homes with outside stairways leading directly from the street to the first floor; that unforgettable view from the

Left: Dame Barbara Hepworth in Trewyn Studio Gardens, spring 1973.

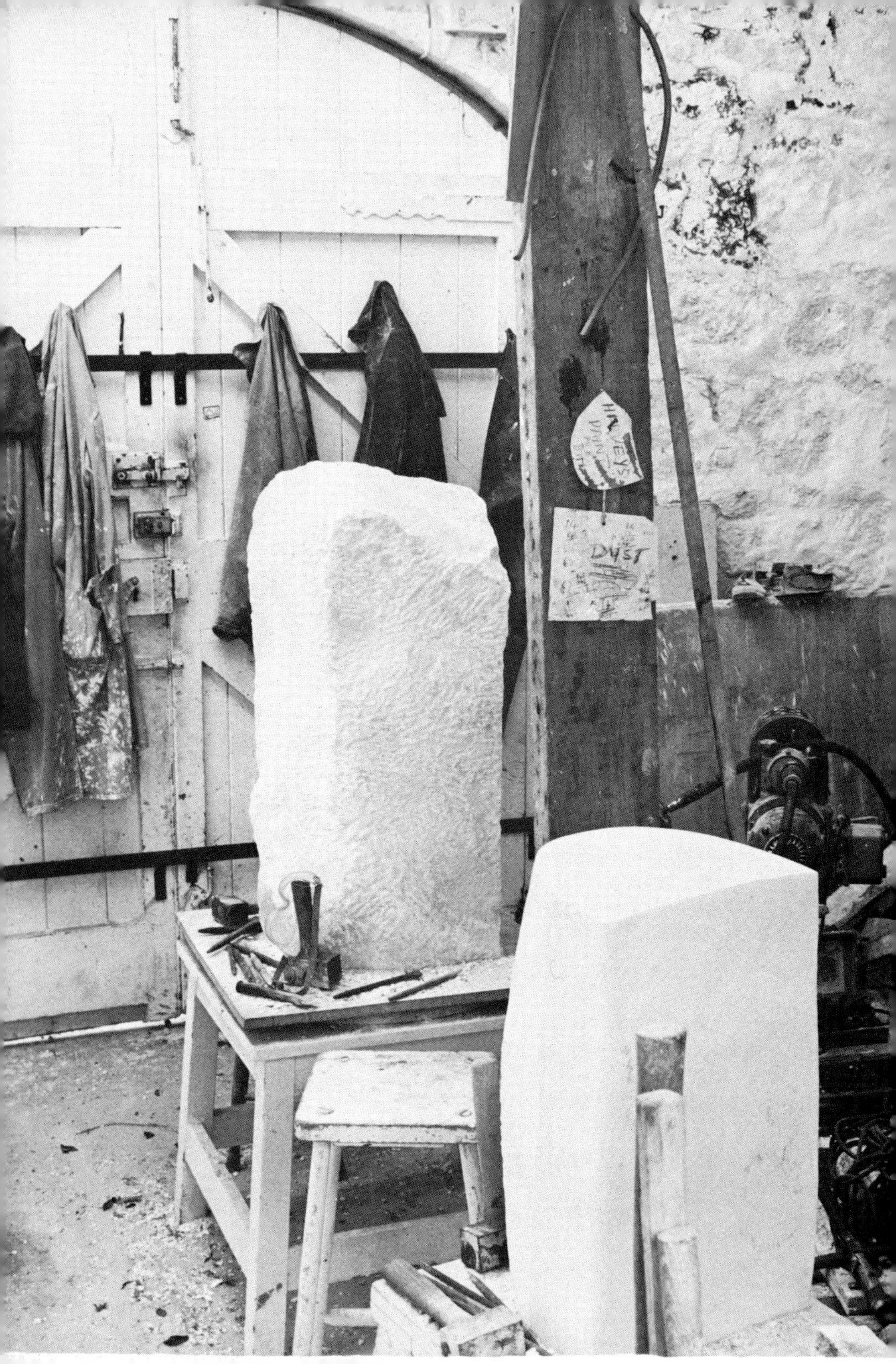
DUST

Left: Unfinished work in Dame Barbara's workshop, virtually unchanged since her death at the age of 72 in 1975.

Below: The first floor at Trewyn: at first a work room, later a bedroom and eventually a sitting-room too. I had two interviews with the sculptor here. 'You won't call me a sculptress, will you?' She made it sound like a question and a condition.

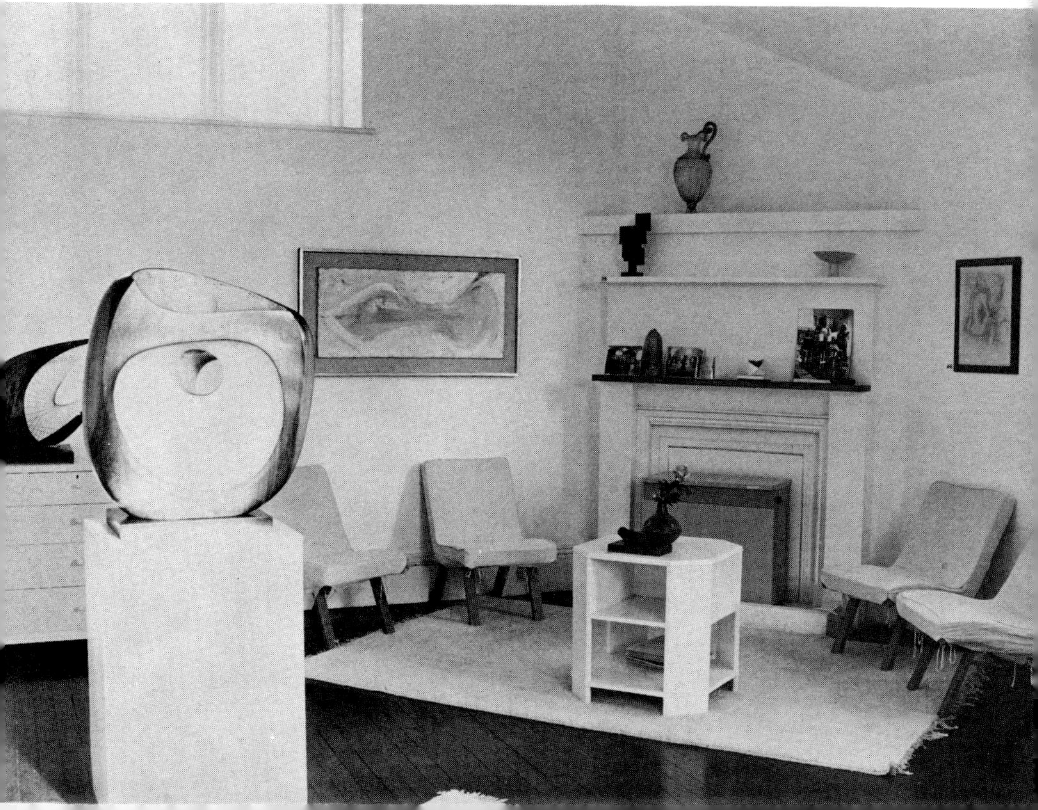

Malakoff, by the bus station, where the streets and the buildings make such fascinating patterns. They could all be taken from a novel: Fish Street, Salubrious Square, Love Lane and Virgin Street; the so-called 'Island', a green hump crowned by St Nicholas's Chapel, seen against the vast blue backcloth of the Atlantic; and, of course, St Ives Bay, your eye easily following its graceful curve with Godrevy Lighthouse—Virginia Woolf's—away in the distance. Commercialisation may have clawed but it has not destroyed.

During the early 1960s, too, I had the luck to interview some fascinating people, years during which I was doing a lot of freelance journalism. One of my greatest strokes of good fortune was when *The Guardian* agreed to a feature on Dame Barbara Hepworth: a decision which enabled me to meet the great lady on two occasions.

Her energy was enormous. In just two interviews I felt her energy flowing like a dynamo.

Barbara Hepworth sculptures: 'let them look at you and they'll speak to you.'

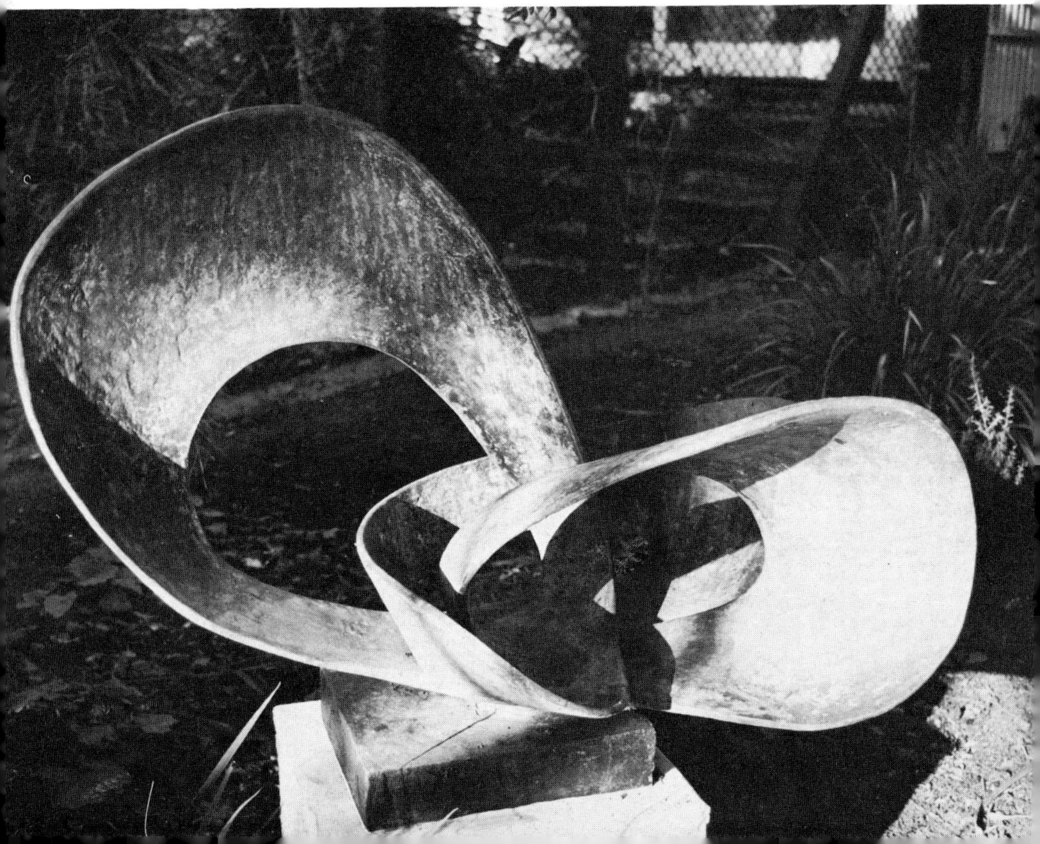

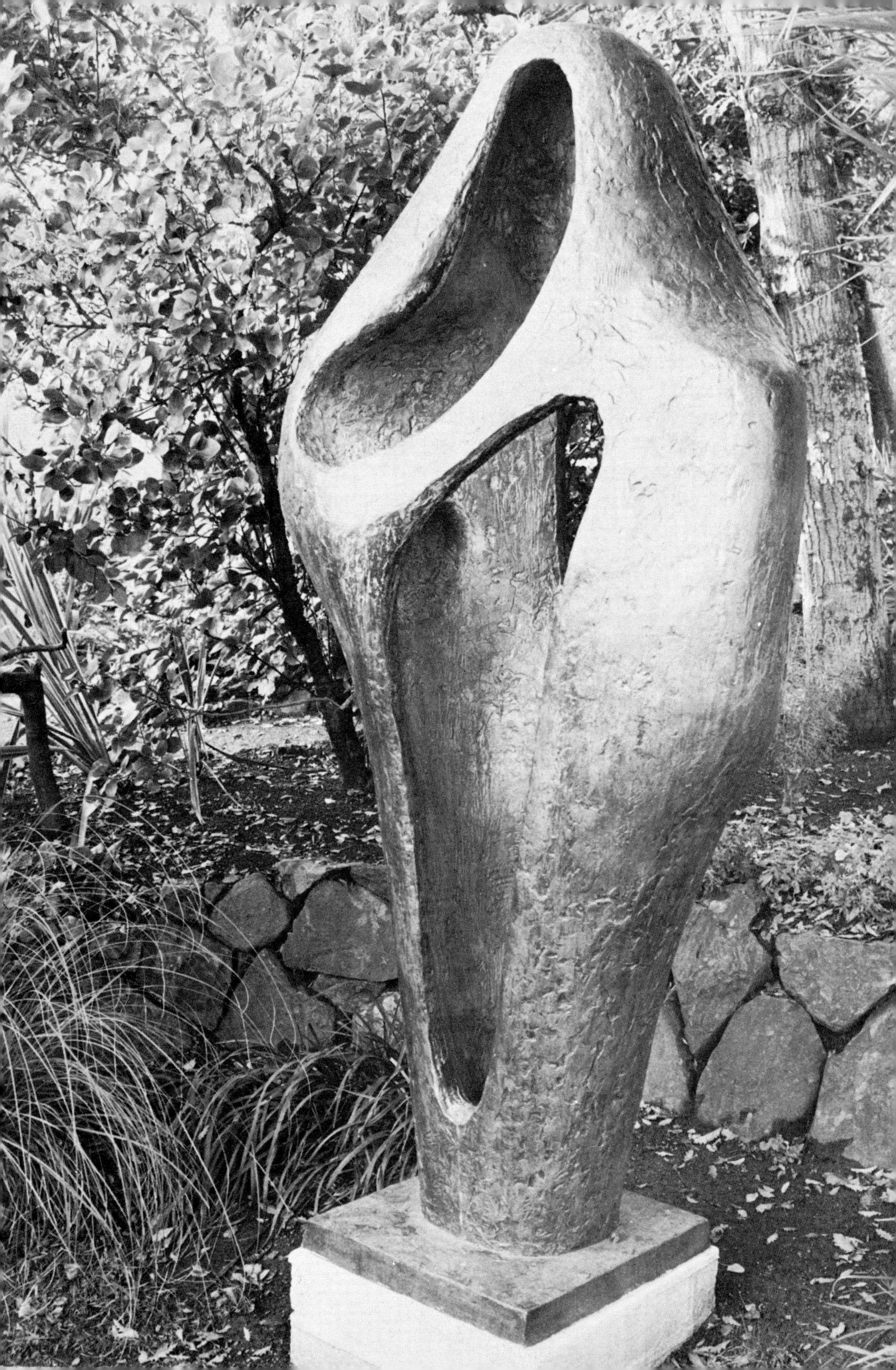

‘Every artist relies on light,’ she told me, ‘and there’s a radiant light here. I’ve only experienced equal brilliance in certain parts of the Mediterranean. I particularly appreciate the softer climate which enables me to work out of doors, away from the stone dust and the artificial light. The artist needs a responsive community too, and here you have just that.’ She had a good opinion of the Cornish: ‘They’re an altogether sophisticated race; they’ve worked abroad as miners; they’ve travelled as sailors . . . they’re very attuned to the universe.’

Of her life and work, she reflected: ‘People think being a sculptor is terribly hard work . . . it can be, but really it’s a matter of rhythm. The physical work is only one side of sculpture; there’s the need for a great deal of thinking, the sorting out of problems. You may have to concentrate hard on a single piece of work for several months. You feel with some things you have managed to transcend material issues, that you have created a thing which looks as though it has grown itself. You’ve transcended human personality. You begin to think that you didn’t make it at all.’

The art critic Bryan Robertson once described her as ‘an energetic supremely disciplined Northcountry woman with an extremely passionate and sensual idea of beauty and life’. She was born in Wakefield, Yorkshire in 1903, the daughter of the county surveyor to the West Riding. She brought up four children, lost one—killed in Korea—married twice, survived the hardship of long early years without recognition or money, and finally established a perfect working environment here at St Ives.

Recalling her beginnings in sculpture: ‘I’ve been unable to think in any other way. I’ve always been thinking of shapes. This is my language. I started tremendously early—at the age of seven—I still recall the immense pleasure of being allowed to make things.’

Dame Barbara saw close parallels between this peninsula and her native West Riding. ‘The landscape in both places possesses a tremendous power. Both places show the same type of scars in industrial developments. The people too have a good deal in common. They have an innate sense of craft. They know how to put a stone in a wall instinctively; it fits just right—and at the first attempt.’

Of her finished works, she said: ‘Some things I am sorry to see go. When I feel like this about a work, and see it again in a new situation, I become rather frightened. I know it’ll be all right, but I’ve left it. It has its own personality . . . I’m outside it now.’

Barbara Hepworth's attitude to tools underlined her sense of vocation—yet she had no hesitation about employing modern instruments.

'I am entirely happy about using modern devices, provided we think of them as means to knowledge and not as means to financial gain. I don't want too many tools, but the sensitive ones are so precious that I can't bear to think of them being touched by anybody else. I see a sensitive tool as an extension of my hand.'

At times she had had to contend with a good deal of criticism—and on occasion open hostility. 'On the whole I managed to feel detached about such criticism. If people say they strongly resent something it means that one is really touching them.'

'What is your attitude to the professional art critic?'

'Either they're right or wrong. If they're right, I learn something. If they're wrong, I'm right.'

Near St Ives Parish Church is Trewyn Studio, formerly her home, and the tropical garden that still houses some of her works. 'Let them look at you and they'll speak to you,' she advised when I confessed I didn't understand all of them. This is now part of the Barbara Hepworth Memorial Museum. She died tragically in a fire at her home in 1975.

The museum, in memory of this gallant, dedicated woman, consists of personal items—letters, photographs, tools and so on—together with wood and stone carvings and paintings and drawings covering the period 1928 to 1974. These items are indoors on two floors. Also inside is a reconstruction of her wood-carving studio showing tools and some unfinished carvings. After seeing these, you are able to wander in her lovely garden where there are some twenty large works, mostly bronze. From the garden, you are able to see into the workshop used for the carving of marble where there are some further unfinished works on view; also the studio used for plaster work.

In addition to the sculptures on view in the museum and the Madonna and Child in the parish church, there are several on view in the town, given to the Borough by Dame Barbara. You will find one in the Public Library, another outside the Guildhall, a third at the Malakoff bus station, and a fourth at the entrance to Longstone Cemetery in Carbis Bay. A carving, owned by the Porthmeor Development Company, is on semi-public display at the entrance to a block of flats known as Piazza in Back Road West.

Barbara Hepworth may be gone, but her influence on this lovely old Cornish town remains, and, for me, more than twenty years on, her brief impact remains a vivid memory—and spur—almost as if it were last week or yesterday.

The garden at Trewyn Studio is very much Dame Barbara Hepworth's creation. Going back more than nine years since her death, I still felt her presence very strongly—so strongly in fact that it was difficult to believe she had gone.

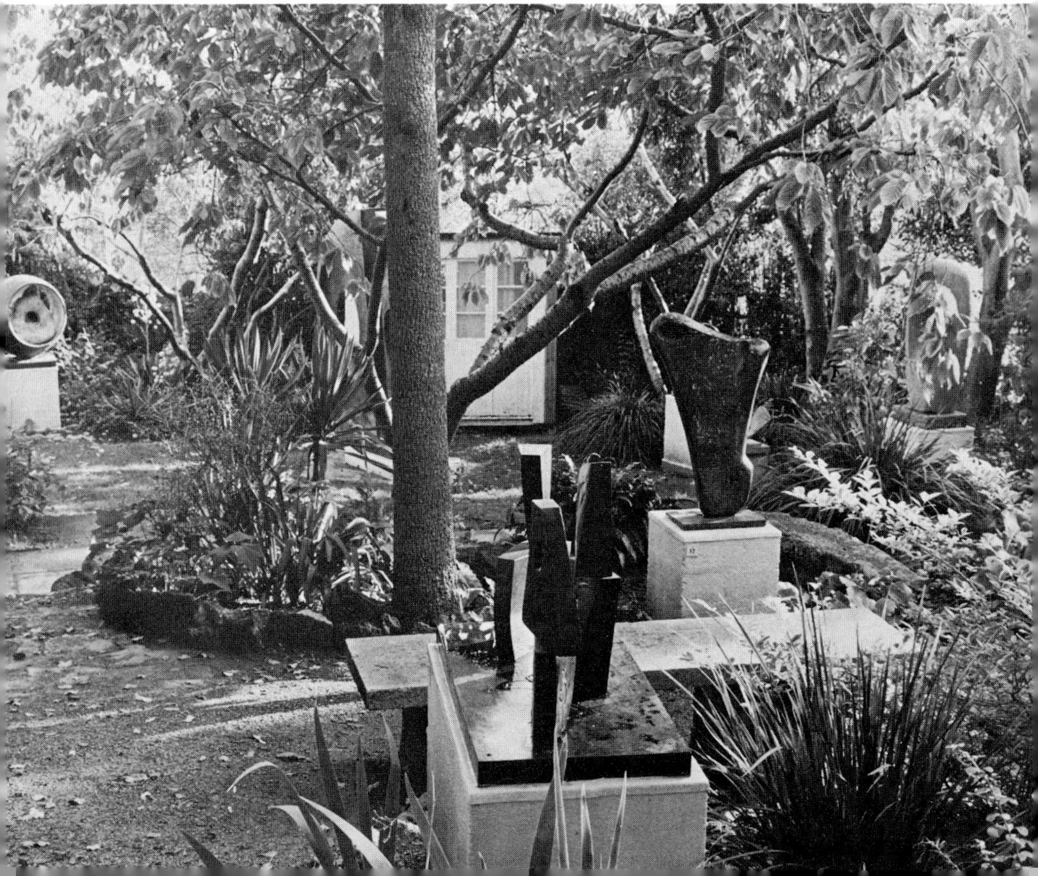

Bernard Leach
St Ives

Another character who will forever be linked with St Ives and its art colony in particular is Bernard Leach, a potter who in the words of the New Zealand critic C. L. Bailey was 'the greatest teacher and the greatest influence there has ever been in the oldest craft known to man'.

Again I was lucky. Early in the 1960s I was doing a series of articles for *The Cornish Magazine* on well-known personalities living and working in Cornwall—and Bernard Leach kindly gave me an interview.

I have never met a more courteous man. He had a statesman-like quality, a breadth of vision and tolerance sometimes lacking in older successful men—he was then in his 76th year. We talked at the Leach Pottery which stands high on the left hand side of the Stennack, that steep hill which climbs out of St Ives and joins that magical memorable coastal road leading on to Zennor where D. H. Lawrence once lived.

I say I have never met a more courteous man, because, one Saturday afternoon, on a visit to the Penwith Gallery in St Ives I witnessed an extraordinary scene. An irate 'philistine' on holiday in Cornwall suddenly turned on the curator with a furious torrent of abuse. 'Call this art,' he shouted, pointing to some of the modern abstracts covering the walls, 'bloody rubbish I call it . . . I wouldn't hang these in a lavatory.'

Bernard Leach happened to be in the gallery. Immediately he came forward to shield the young lady sitting in the hot seat behind the desk. With great dignity and calm, and without a hint of condescension he 'tried' to put forward a case for modern and the need for a gallery to embrace different talents—including different ways of looking at the world.

It was, of course, an impossible task, for the bigot just would not listen or try to see the other point of view. As he disappeared, red-faced and puffing, into Back Road West, I wondered if he realised he had just been talking with the greatest potter in the world.

I reminded Bernard Leach of the encounter when we met at his pottery. He remembered it and just smiled.

'I was born in Hong Kong on the 5 January 1887,' he told me. 'I originally planned to be a painter and studied at the Slade School of Art. Experiences in other schools followed and, for my sins, I spent a year in a bank.

'My father, an English Colonial Judge, didn't approve of my ambitions in art. It wasn't quite respectable to be a painter in those days. "Bernard, can't you think of something else?" he asked. And my stepmother was even more shocked *and* expressed herself candidly.

'Inspired by the writings of Lafcadio Hearn, I went out to Japan in 1909. "Why was their art so different? What were their roots?" I wanted to find out the answers to these questions.'

Like Saul's conversion on the road to Damascus, Bernard Leach's conversion to pottery was a sudden shaft of light. 'One afternoon' he recalls 'I was invited to a Japanese tea party. There were about a dozen painters, actors and potters squatting on the floor, painting pots. They invited me to join them, and within an hour I had been carried into another world. At once I decided to find a master, and the sixth Kenzan became that master. I never attempted to work in his style but he taught me the ABC of pottery. Day after day on the bare boards of his humble home I learned my alphabet of clay.

'Then in 1920 I returned to England. Chance or fate brought me to Cornwall. There was a Craft Guild here, run by a lady of some financial background, and she wanted a potter. Somebody suggested that I should apply for the job. I did, and got it.

'Cornwall has influenced my work, of course, but one is apt to overwrite it. One forgets stern winters, like the one we are experiencing; one forgets the lack of adjoining counties; and one forgets that these people are not Englishmen, but Celts. Although I don't come from Cornwall, I feel more at home here than in any other place. I'm drawn to its granite bastions . . . and to the imaginative Celt.'

Bernard Leach was the first western potter to train in the Orient, and his pots represent a synthesis of western and eastern ideas. The Japanese potter Shoji Hamada accompanied him to St Ives and they worked together here for three years. Over the years, too, there

Bernard Leach: 'Cornwall has influenced my work . . . Although I don't come from Cornwall, I feel more at home here than in any other place. I'm drawn to its granite bastions . . . and to the imaginative Celt.'

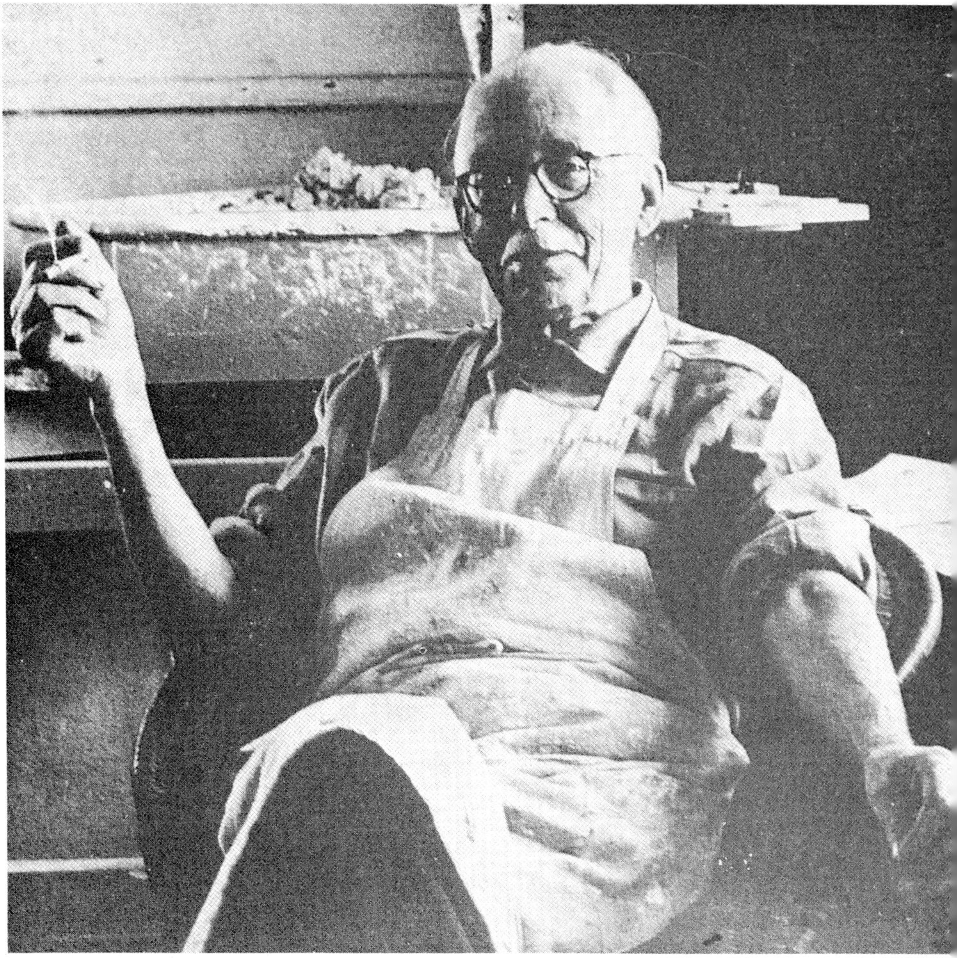

has been an interchange of visits, exhibitions and ideas between St Ives and Japan. Indeed this tradition continued in 1956 when Bernard Leach married his wife Janet who had been studying with Hamada and in the rural potteries for two years.

During the course of that cold grey January afternoon, he took me round his pottery. It was a new world for me—I had never seen pots come to life before—and felt as if one of the Gods was taking me on a conducted tour of his Empire. The sheer speed of the operation astonished: a pot becoming a personality inside something less than five minutes.

'Here in the pottery, we have adopted the Cornish motto "one and all" ' he explained, 'and by making a "we job" instead of an "I job" we have solved our economic problem . . . hand-workers in a machine age.' His warmth and enthusiasm were infectious. 'It's *still* possible for a group of people, even a very varied group, to find and give satisfaction because they believe in their work and each other.'

Only four years short of his 80th birthday, Bernard Leach was

St Ives, a town that has inspired more fine painting than almost anywhere else outside London, and a good deal of writing too.

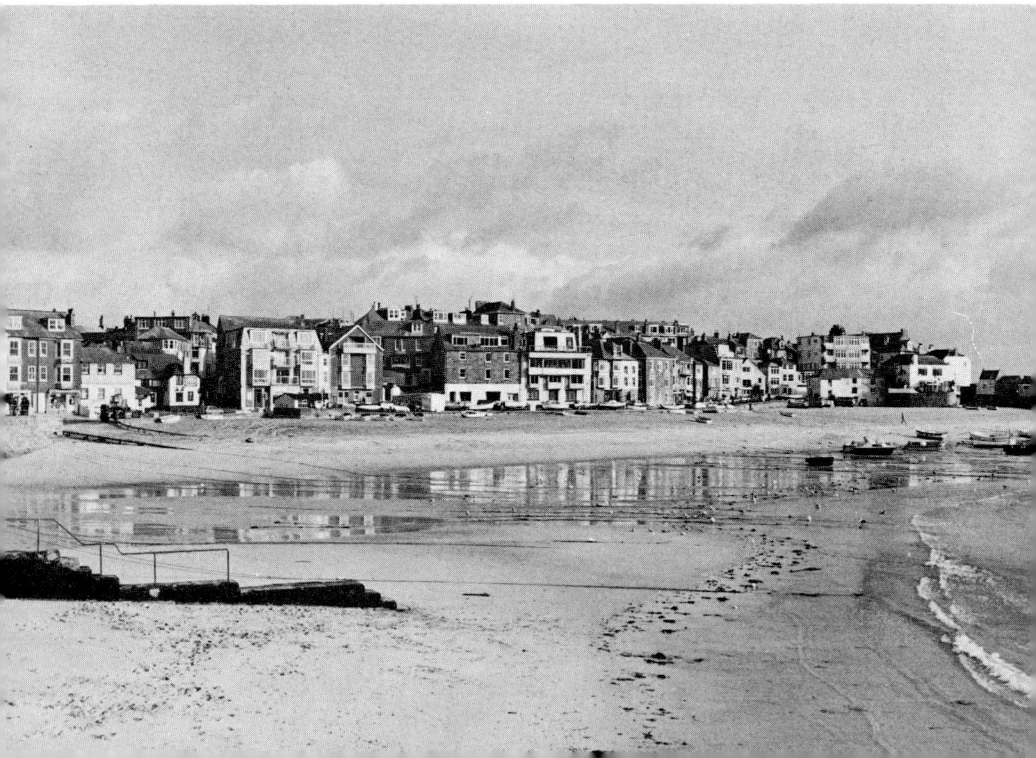

still working every day: 'I've kept a regular pattern and throughout my life I can say I've worked hard. Naturally, one tends to ease off a little at my stage of life, but I hope to go on making many more pots. The artist, of course, never stops working. He's still at it even when he's away from the workshop; he works in his dreams, he works in his daydreams. If I'm sitting in a train, I'm still at it. That drawer over there, is full of sketches, things scribbled on the backs of envelopes, and odd bits of paper. Very seldom do I sit and stare.'

He saw pottery as a marriage of sculpture and painting, a special kind of abstraction.

'How do you see a pot?' I asked.

'Now that's a good question. Form first, (a long pause), no, I think material even before form. So much depends on the material, the quality of the clay and its determination of form and pattern. One sees a pot as a living thing. *Life and vitality*, that's the simple criterion.'

I thought of his reply ten years later when I came across an article by Noel Welch in Denys Val Baker's *Cornish Review*. She wrote:

'I was not prepared for the vitality; I should have been, it is in the pots. For the warmth, the directness, yes. I had once sat next to Bernard Leach at a Penwith party. Now, his sheer vigour took me by surprise. It explains why, at eighty-six, he is about to bring out his first book of poems and to make his eleventh visit to Japan. He has ascended to age, gathering strength with every step.

'I first set eyes on Leach pots one summer afternoon in 1953 when I idly dropped in at the pottery on the hill above St Ives. Once it was where the town ended, beyond being nothing but farms and sea. The sun seemed to have stroked the outside of every pot in a different way. I took home a large bowl with a deep spreading glow on its slightly rough exterior; inside, it was the cool, satisfying green of a cabbage leaf. Later, this bowl found its way to a very grand London room full of marble tables, Persian carpets, wine silk curtains; there was even a golden goblet—it was not my room. The bowl was as at home as on the scrubbed deal table in my studio.'

In that conversation in 1963, he reflected: 'In this age of ours there are very few people who get the chance of making the most of their talents, of doing the things they really enjoy. As a people we are starved of feeling, intuition and imagination in our day-to-day life. We have become lop-sided creatures, bending over our desks and benches, compensating with vicarious pleasures outside our work. By contrast a potter uses his natural faculties of heart, head and hand in balance—he is a whole man. His, in fact, is a way of life.'

But he was optimistic about the future: 'Education is beginning to tackle the problem. Schools today offer more opportunities. In my days at school we only used our hands to catch a cricket ball or a football, using them for any other purpose was unthinkable, somehow rather degrading.'

Towards the end of our conversation, I reminded him that, ten years earlier, somebody had written something to the effect that Bernard Leach, despite all his accomplishments, regarded himself essentially as a student of his subject.

'Do you *still* consider yourself a student?' I asked.

'Yes,' he replied. 'I'm still very much a student. After all, one is dealing with an infinity.'

The next day I wrote thanking him for his time and hospitality and above all, for 'opening a new door of experience'.

He replied, by return with courtesy saying he had enjoyed our meeting, adding, 'There is no greater privilege in life than opening a door.'

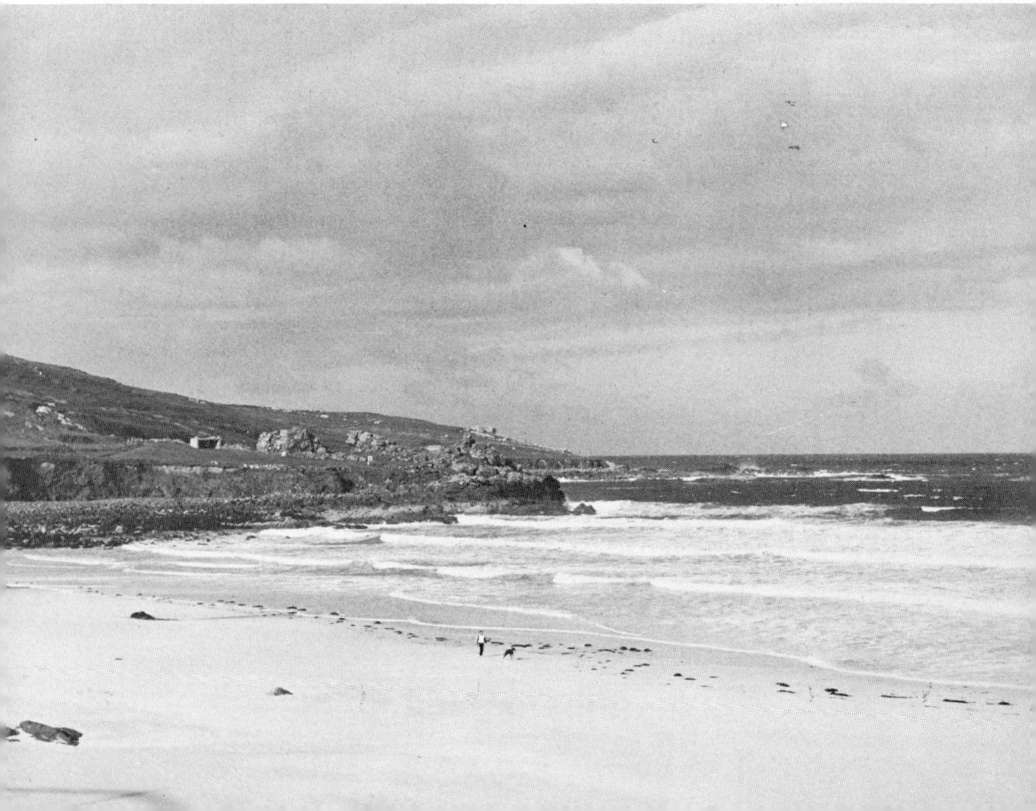

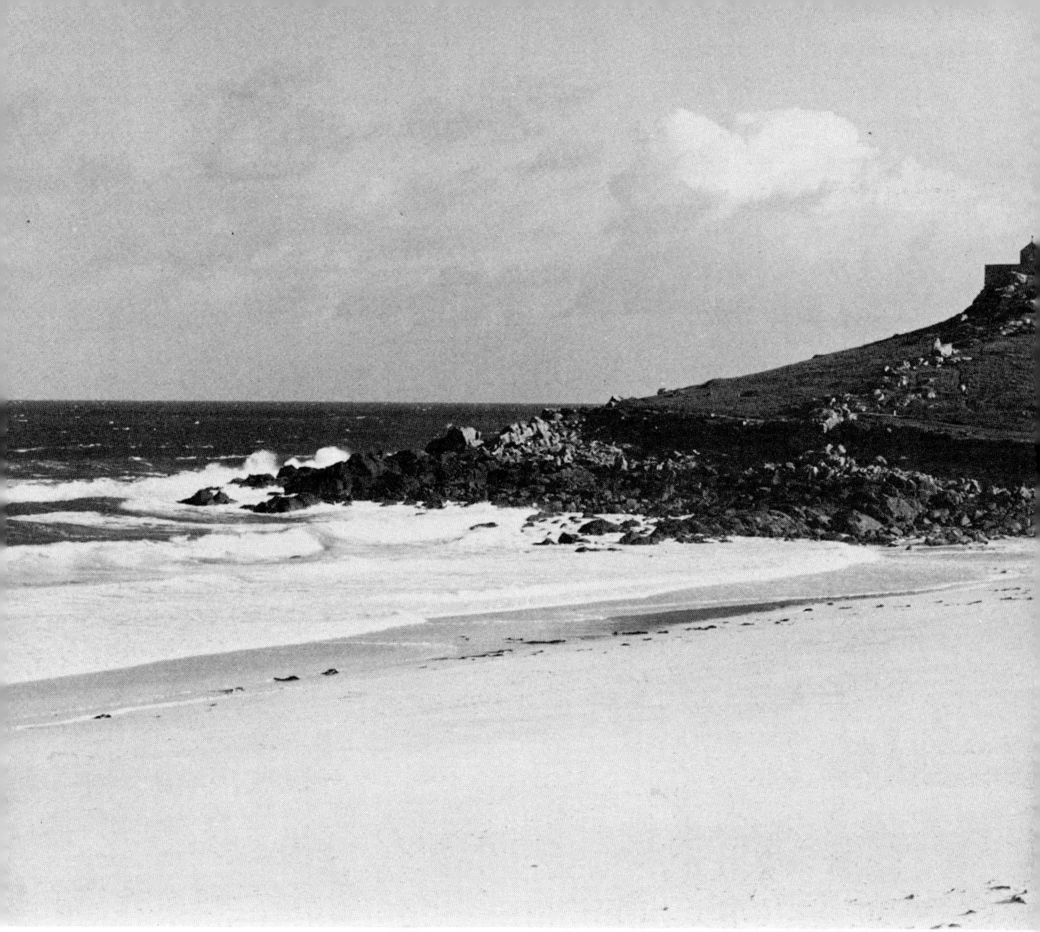

Two faces of Porthmeor Beach, St Ives, on a Saturday morning in October. Few Westcountry resorts can boast such a lovely stretch of sand.

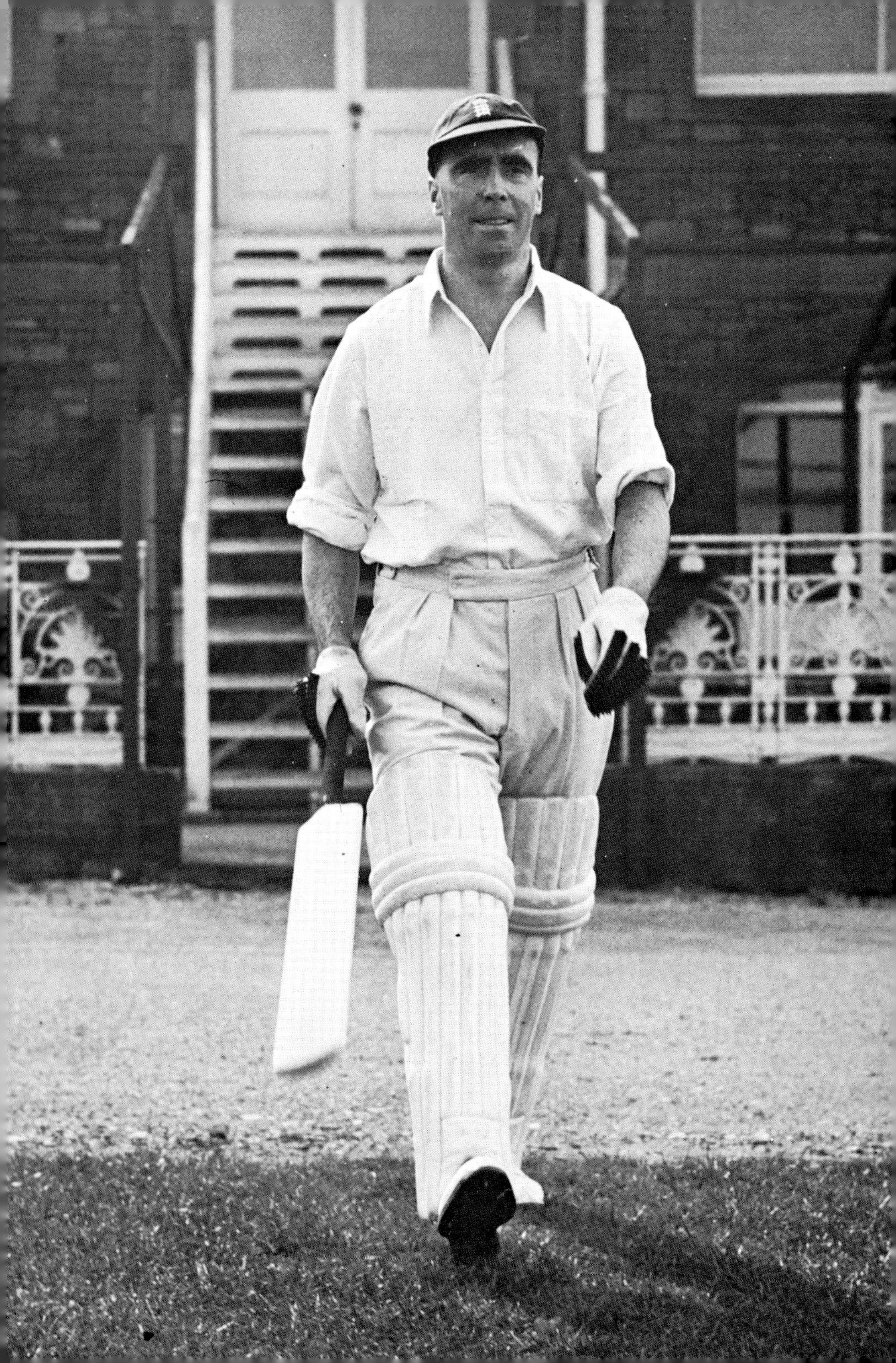

Jack Crapp
St Columb

St Columb is a stronghold of Cornish Hurling, that ancient sport which was almost certainly the ancestor of our modern game of Rugby.

Hurling's origin lies deep in Cornwall's past, vague and hazy like the landscape itself on a murky morning. Some scholars believe it stems from the Bronze Age. Times were when it was a popular sport, but the negative Puritans condemned it, and today St Columb is its last real stronghold.

In 1823 a boy, William Webb Ellis by name, picked up the ball, and broke the law by running with it, on the turf of Rugby School, thereby creating the modern game of Rugby Football. Here in Cornwall, though, we feel justified in claiming that our Hurlers were the real pioneers, for an account of the sport by Richard Carew in 1602 uncannily anticipated some of Rugby's laws and patterns by more than two centuries. There is, however, a basic difference between Hurling and Rugby in that the objective in Hurling is to take the ball back into your own goal, or alternatively to carry it over the Parish boundary.

St Columb is a distinctive town, too, thanks to the architecture of William White. White's St Columb Rectory with its moat, and sixteenth-century Trewan Hall, which he restored, and his bank built in 1857—now a solicitor's office—are only some of his buildings, all giving the district a character of its own.

But whenever I travel through its narrow streets, my thoughts are usually far from Hurling and William White's architecture. Instead I am often thinking of Jack Crapp, the first Cornishman to

Left: Jack Crapp coming out to bat on the County Ground at Bristol.

have played for England in a test match—until 1984 he was the *only* Cornishman to wear an England cap.

It is a curious fact that whereas Cornwall has produced a whole host of fine Rugby players, as many as twenty-eight England internationals—admittedly not all of them natives—Jack Crapp was the solitary Cornishman in English test cricket for more than a hundred years.

John Frederick Crapp was born at St Columb Major—not the same place as St Columb Minor—on 14 October 1912. He moved to Bristol in 1921, but I like to think as a small boy he was taken to the hurling matches in Cornwall, and that he played his first primitive cricket hereabouts.

Jack Crapp did, in fact, play for St Columb a few times. 'As a young man on holiday to Cornwall,' his old friend Harold Walkey told me, 'I remember on one occasion we had this match at Roche, and we cycled all the way there . . . including Jack. He made some runs, but we thought he got a rough decision when he was given out. "It was all right," said Jack when he came off the field. "Before that I was out at least four times!" '

The Gloucestershire cricketer clearly had a great affection for the area. 'He holidayed with us for many years,' Harold Walkey recalled. 'He was a grand chap, and but for the death of his father in the 1914-1918 war, he may never have moved to Bristol. His mother, a Bristolian, probably thought the boys had a better chance in Bristol than in Cornwall.'

In 1936 Jack Crapp made a considerable leap from Club into first-class County Cricket, joining Gloucestershire straight from Stapleton Cricket Club. Grahame Parker, the Gloucestershire historian, in his fine book *Gloucestershire Road*, wrote: 'Crapp . . . demonstrated the great strength of Bristol club cricket by making one thousand and fifty two runs in his first season. A left-handed, middle order batsman, phlegmatic to a degree with a wistful sense of humour, of great patience and sure technique, a fine slip fielder, his place was assured for many years to come.'

In the Bristol pavilion one afternoon, an old Gloucestershire member, learning that I was a Cornishman, and living only a few miles from Jack Crapp's birthplace, told me how Jack came to join the County Club. Apparently Harry Smith, the Gloucestershire coach, couldn't make up his mind about the young Cornishman, and took the great W. R. Hammond along to watch him in action. Wally

Hammond had no doubts. 'Get his signature,' he said, 'and don't waste your time coaching him, he doesn't need it.' It's a good story, and I like to think it's true.

In a career which stretched from the summer of 1936—Hitler robbed him, like many others, of golden years—Jack Crapp's achievements for the county of the Graces, Jessop and Hammond were substantial. He went to the wicket for Gloucestershire on 708 occasions, scoring over 22,000 runs, averaging 34.84—and holding as many as 366 catches. He scored his 1,000 runs in the season no less than fourteen times, providing the middle order stability to many a Gloucestershire innings. In all, he made 39 centuries, and for England he managed an average of 29.

His test appearances for England were restricted to seven matches, and he had the misfortune to meet Messrs Ray Lindwall and Keith Miller, at the height of their fame and fury—a combination which many shrewd judges rate as the finest opening attack of all time.

He earned his first test cap on the strength of a carefully built 100 not out against Bradman's 1948 Australians at Bristol. 'Well done, Jack,' said the generous Keith Miller, 'but watch your head in the test.' It was a curious prophecy too, for in the test match Crapp was 'felled' by a Lindwall bouncer, having 'lost the ball in the crowd', but courageously he refused to come off the field. Not the luckiest of cricketers, he went to India during the winter of 1953-54 with a very good Commonwealth team, but had to return home through illness after only two matches.

Outside his considerable record as a player, Jack Crapp holds a special place in Gloucestershire cricket history: the county's first professional captain. David Foot, writing of him in his book *From Grace to Botham*, reflected, 'He was not dynamic or madly imaginative; but he possessed Cornish commonsense, and was liked by his players. In fact, he was the cricketer everyone liked . . .' Sadly, eczema which plagued him for so long, forced him to give up the captaincy after the 1954 season and he retired in 1956.

Thereafter he served cricket faithfully as an umpire, rising to test match rank. He umpired rather as he had batted. To quote Grahame Parker, 'His quiet bearing and slow, understanding smile cooled many a tricky situation.'

No more dedicated man ever wore the white coat. Bill Andrews, that great Somerset cricketing character, told me of just one

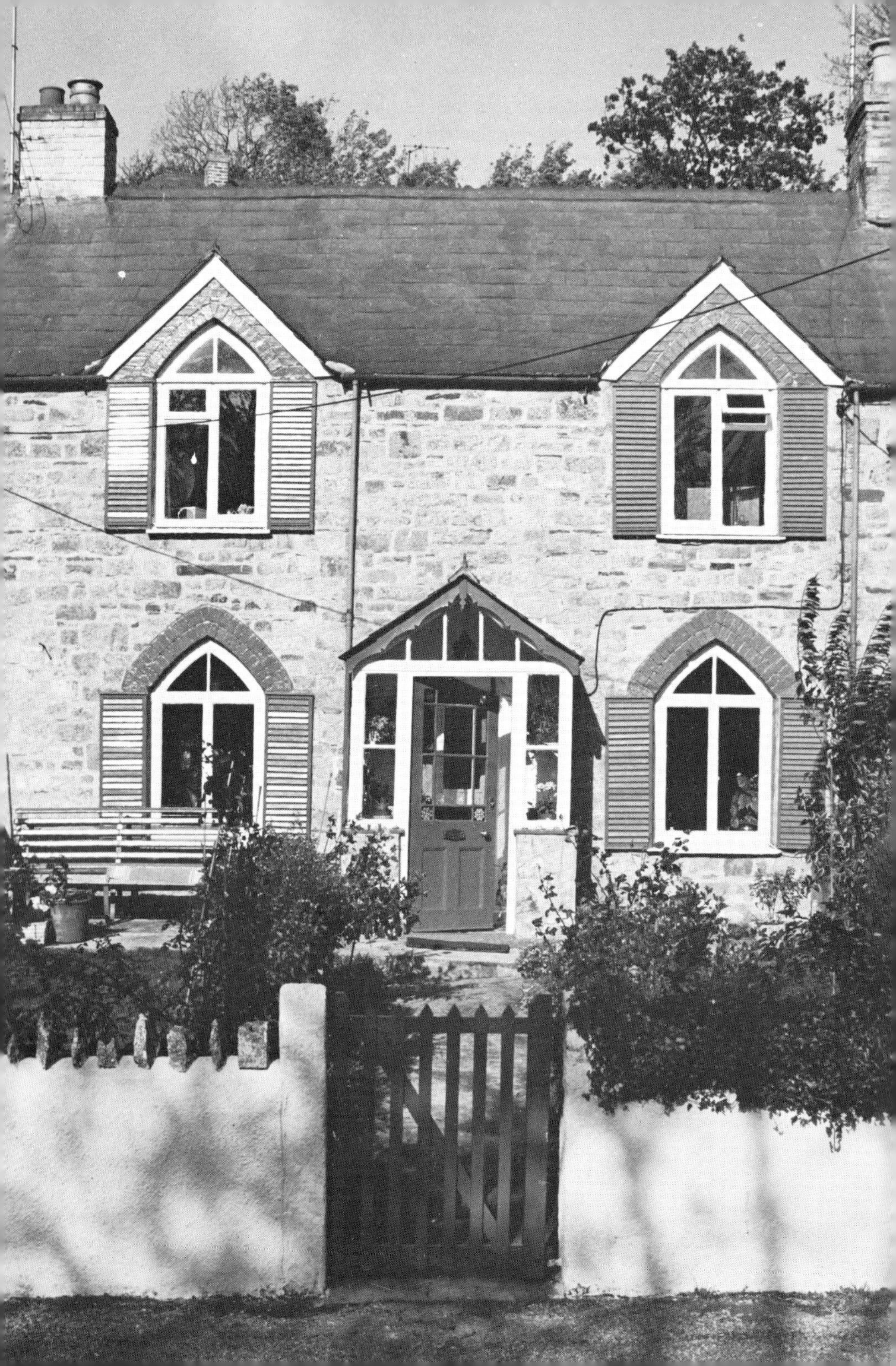

example. Bill, incidentally, had a very high opinion of Jack Crapp as an umpire, but on this occasion there was a rare error. 'Somerset were playing Kent at Weston-super-Mare,' Bill recalled, 'and it was a very important match for the South African Terry Barwell. He had been brought back into the team after a bad spell, and a lot depended on his performance as to whether the county would retain him. Unluckily for him, Jack gave him out LBW before he had scored. Terry told me he had got the faintest of touches before being hit on the pad. Twelve months later I met Jack in Bristol and he immediately asked, "Did Terry Barwell touch that ball at Clarence Park last year, Bill?" When I told him, he was very upset. He had been watching the bowler's feet very closely and, for once, had been a fraction late looking up, and saw Barwell, on the back foot, plumb. Jack was deeply upset . . . even a year later.'

I met Jack Crapp only once, in his umpiring days, when Alan Gibson introduced us as 'two fellow Cornishmen' and we had a drink in the Grace Room at Bristol. He wanted me to talk about Cornwall, and I wanted to hear him on cricket, but, for me, it was still a memorable meeting. Now, too, I regret I did not see him play more often.

Some called him dour—and he often was, battling to save his team, but he could unleash strokes if an innings needed acceleration—capable of being Cavalier or Roundhead according to the needs of his side. I can still see him in my mind's eye: the watchful batsman at the crease or crouched at slip, ready for those snicks from the outside edge of the bat.

Alan Gibson, that most elegant of essayists, pinned Jack Crapp beautifully to paper in *The Cricketer* in 1980 when he wrote: 'He is a quiet, gentle man: not one of the fiery Cornishmen. He would not have done in the back row of the scrum in a Cornwall-Devon match, when the Redruth crowd was getting worked up, and Vic Roberts of England and Harlequins was waving his forces on, all in a howl of black and gold. In his early years, Jack had the reputation of being a cautious batsman. That was partly because he spent so much time batting with Hammond, and Hammond's Gloucestershire partners did not usually get much bowling. In his later years, after the war,

Left: St Columb cottage where Jack Crapp was born. He did in fact play for St Columb a few times.

when I saw him often, he was full of strokes, not all of them orthodox, and was inclined to lose his wicket with a genial hoick towards long-on (he was left-handed, at least as a batsman—I cannot remember ever seeing him bowl).'

Towards the end of the 1984 season I attended a cricket sale in the same Grace Room. They were selling his old England blazers and his cricket bag. It was too painful to handle them, let alone think of bidding for them and I left before the sale began.

Coming back to Cornwall that evening, I wondered what had happened to his cricket boots. The legend goes—and people who should know tell me it's true—that, after his first season with Gloucestershire—deputising for Hammond in the opening match he scored 66 against Oxford University—tall Tom Goddard took him to one side. 'Jack, my boy,' he said, 'it looks as if you're going to be playing for us for a long, long time. Take my advice, and buy yourself a decent pair of boots.'

Apparently Jack did just that, and wore them for the rest of his cricketing life, including his years as an umpire.

In his modest gentlemanly way, Jack Crapp was a great ambassador for both cricket and Cornwall.

F.T. Glasscock
Tintagel

I never met Frederick Thomas Glasscock.

That might be just as well. All of me would like to have met him, but a good half tells me I would not have liked the whole man or, more accurately, my face may not have fit.

He died when I was only one year old, and when I came to live at Bossiney, hard by Tintagel in the mid '60s, he was just a misty figure from the '20s and '30s.

Curiously, though, today I feel I know him fairly well. But that could be an illusion because, deep down, I doubt if many—or any—local people knew him *well*. He was, in a way, a mystery man, a kind of Arthurian legend. Yet the paradox is there because, in a material sense, in his lifetime he was 'Mr Tintagel', and, to this day, he has left a remarkable legacy to North Cornwall.

Tintagel main street is no architectural gem, but it does contain one delightful surprise. Hiding behind a gift-shop frontage is a real Arthurian experience. Beyond the shop are two halls, conceived by this rich eccentric character.

Everything here is based on the Arthurian romances. This was, at one time, the headquarters of the Fellowship of the Order of the Round Table, an organisation pioneered by Frederick Thomas Glasscock. A millionaire—partner in the famous custard firm of Monkhouse and Glasscock—he came to Cornwall to retire, but instead, falling in love with the romances and seeing their commercial possibilities, he founded the order and started reaping a second fortune. He died in 1934, aboard the *Queen Mary*, on his way to the United States.

Some people may say the Hall of Chivalry is overdone but for many visitors here this building represents a wonderful introduction to the whole Arthurian saga.

Today the Hall is used for Masonic Lodge meetings. Colour and

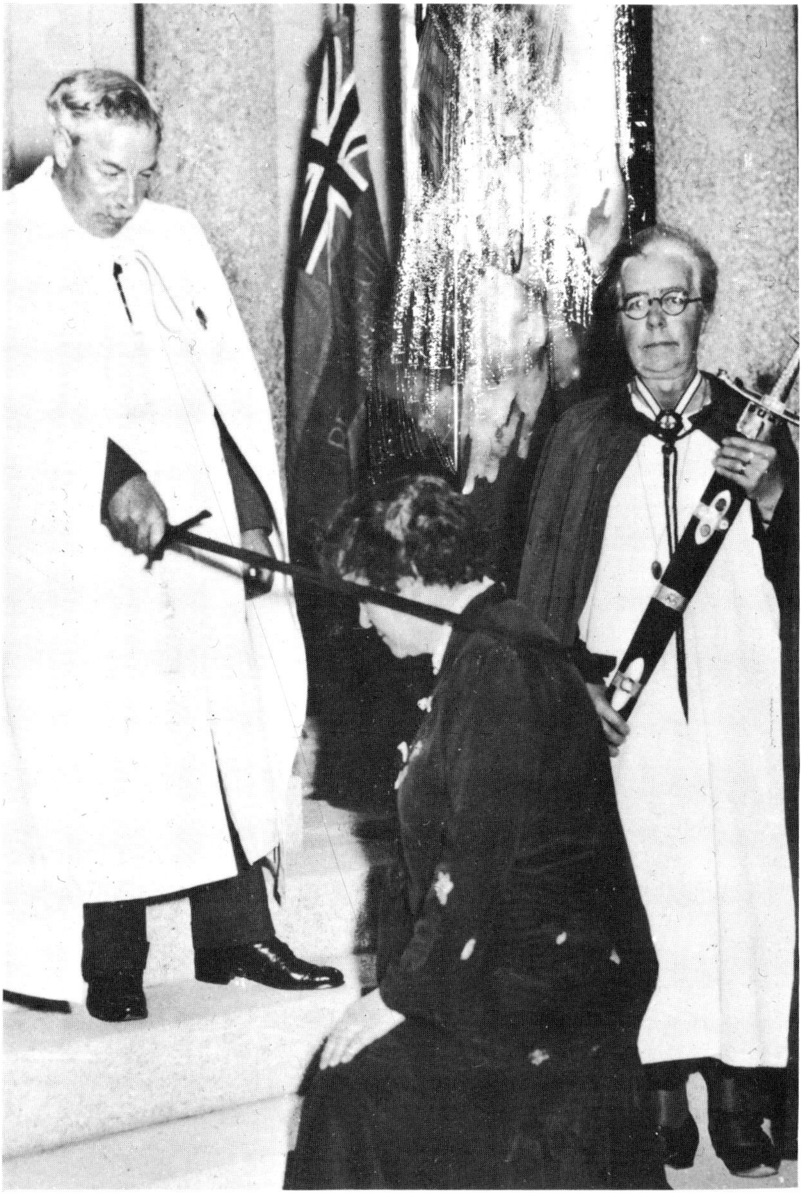

light make great impact. The stones are astonishing in their variety, subtle shades, contrasting differences. Green, blue, grey, brown, buff, cream, golden, pink, silver-grey, white, red, black and yellow—you begin to comprehend Cornwall's mineral wealth—and the windows are coloured in such a way as to reflect their virtues. Those portraying the highest spiritual qualities are brightest. The colours also correspond with the rainbow: purple at one end, golden red at the other. Shading and lighting, allied to curtains stretching from ceiling to the floor, give the impression that you are moving from comparative darkness into a beautiful and brilliant glow.

Ronald Youlton who still lives in Tintagel remembers when Frederick Glasscock first came to the village. He was a teenager when the retired millionaire saw a display of Monkhouse and Glasscock's jellies and custard powders in the window of his father's grocer's shop—a display that also included the sword Excalibur and the Round Table, which first caught the imagination of Frederick Glasscock.

Ronald Youton recalled: 'He built a small hall at first, about 1930, but when his Fellowship of the Order of the Knights of the Round Table flourished, a larger hall was needed.

'You could join the Order as a Searcher if you were a child. A teenager could be a pilgrim for a small fee. You could then progress through twelve months' probation to qualify as a knight, as long as you were proposed and seconded. You were then presented with a book on the Fellowship and other literature for a small cost.

'The King Arthur business snowballed and on 5 June 1933 over 500 people came from all parts for the opening of the new grand Hall of Chivalry, built behind the earlier King Arthur's Hall. This was consecrated by the Bishop of Truro and Frederick Glasscock was well on the way to making his second million. He went to America and launched the idea successfully over there and on his return had to employ secretaries to deal with the growing correspondence.'

'What sort of person was Frederick Glasscock?'

Ronald Youlton remembered him clearly:

'He was short, very precise and domineering—a self-made man who behaved rather like a little god. But he was a great benefactor

Left: Frederick Glasscock knights a pilgrim. 'He was a self-made man who behaved rather like a god.'

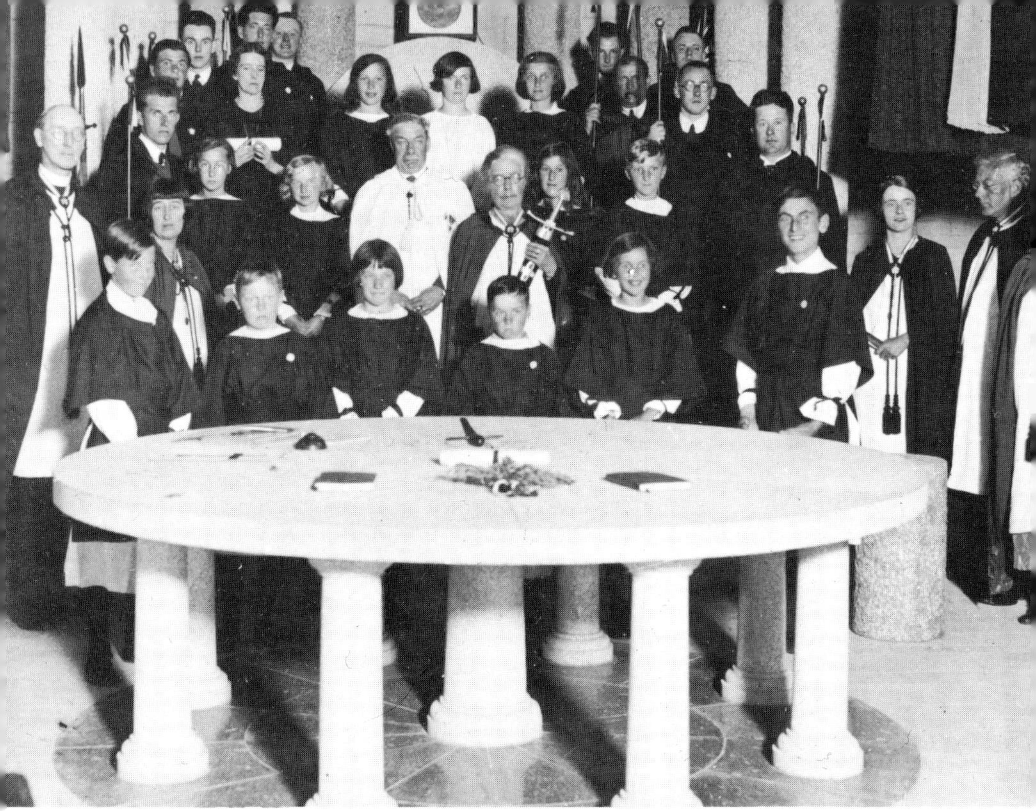

Searchers, Pilgrims and Knights at the Round Table.

to Tintagel, providing the men's club, tennis courts, roller skating, starting scout and guide troops. So most people in the village were prepared to go along with him.'

Ronald Youlton, who himself started as a Pilgrim in the Order, went on to describe the knighting ceremony: 'The new knight would be suitably attired, while those already knighted wore robes of blue or red according to their rank, whether knights of the sword or sceptre. The principles of the Order were read from a scroll, prayers were said, oaths made. The ceremony started in semi-darkness until the sword Excalibur was drawn from the scabbard with a great flourish and Glasscock—in the role of King Arthur—struck the new knight on the shoulder, giving him his name: Sir Galahad, perhaps, Sir Lancelot, or Sir Bedivere.'

I later talked to William Charles Grose, a Tintagel businessman in his seventies, who bathes in the Atlantic off Bossiney all round the calendar. It was his father who drew up the plans for first the Eirenikon, Mr Glasscock's former residence, and later the Hall of Chivalry.

'Though my father was not an architect, Mr Glasscock obviously had great faith in him,. It all began in the 1914-18 War when Mr Glasscock stayed at the Castle Hotel and ran his custard empire business from there with his secretary. He decided to settle in Tintagel, and asked my father, Charles Grose, to become general factotum. Father was a carpenter, painter and undertaker, and sub-contracted a good deal of the work. Most of the stone that went into the building of the Eirenikon came from Trebrea Lodge Quarry. I can still see stone being carted down the lane by horse and cart. The building cost was somewhere around £24,000.

'They were good employers, the Glasscocks at the Eirenikon. When workmen were working on the extensions there, at 11 o'clock in the morning and again at 3 o'clock in the afternoon there was always

'It all began in the 1914-18 War when Mr Glasscock stayed at the Castle Hotel . . .'

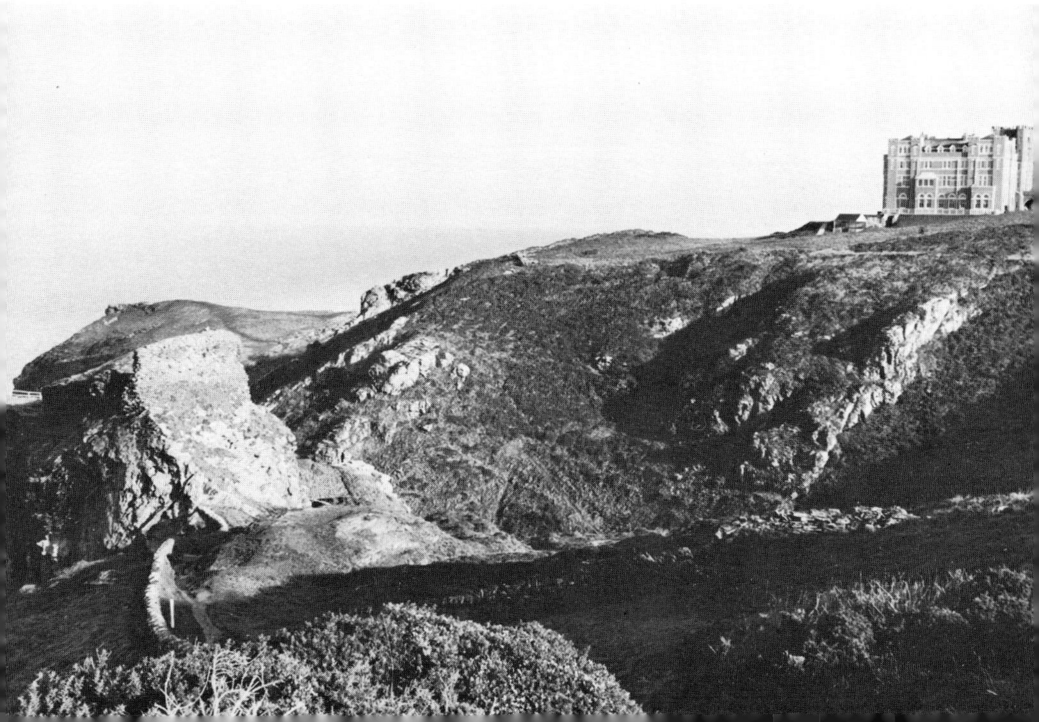

tea and cake for all of them—no matter how many men were on site— and Mrs Glasscock had the habit of calling everybody "Lovey".

'Mr Glasscock never, to my knowledge, ever asked for an estimate. He might say, "Mr Grose, if we add this or that, what will it cost?" But he never asked for a definite price. He never liked to see people idling, though. I remember, one day at the Hall of Chivalry, he came around with a local lady friend and I was holding a sheet of material for another workman, and he barked out: "Don't look when a lady lifts her skirt!" I wasn't looking of course—it was his way of saying "Get on with your job!". On another occasion, we had an electrician from Plymouth, an out-and-out Communist. One day he started singing *The Red Flag* and Mr Glasscock heard him . . there was all Hell to pay . . . I thought he was going to throw him out but he didn't *and* we didn't hear any more *Red Flag*.

'But for all that Mr Glasscock was a generous man. I know for a fact he arranged with butcher Teague to send regular joints of beef to families who had husbands unemployed. He told me that he had once been a barefooted boy in London, who was glad to have a kipper for tea.

The Eirenikon—Glasscock's home in Tintagel . . .

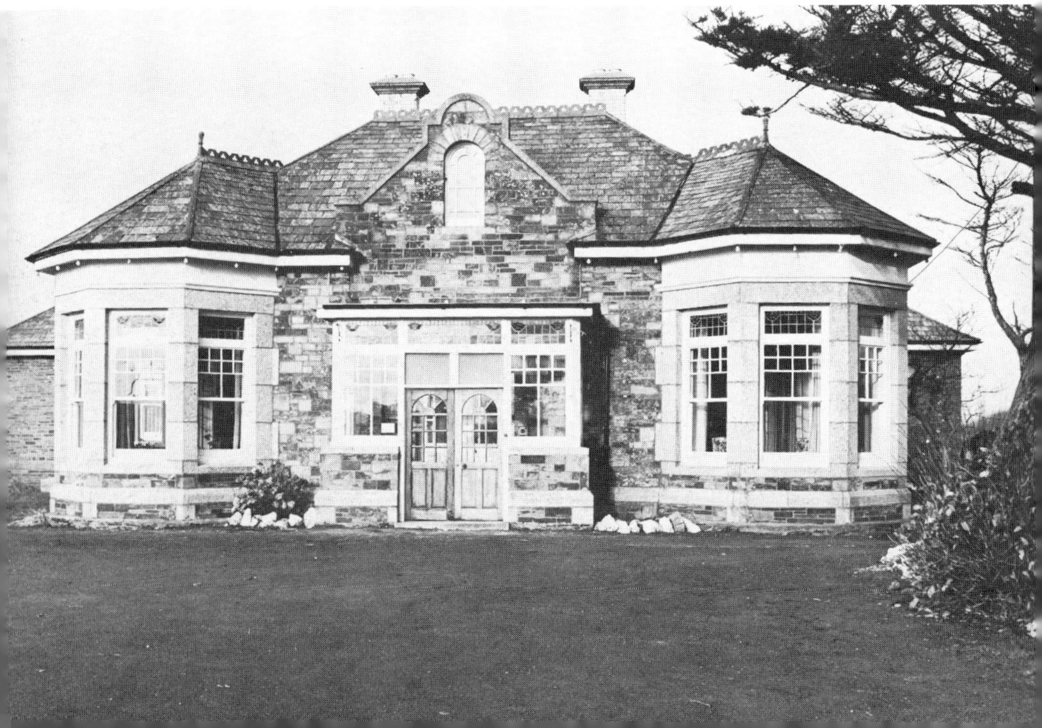

'He was a curious mixture. If your face fitted, then you were in, and all was well . . . but if it didn't then that was that. If you were invited to play tennis at the Eirenikon then you were expected to turn up on time and to be decently turned out . . . and that went for all his functions.'

One Tintagel resident who has long and fond memories of the Glasscock family is Ada Florence Sinclair whose late husband Eddie was on Mr Glasscock's staff. 'The family link goes back a long way,' she explained to me, 'as my mother was housekeeper for the Glasscocks when they lived in Forest Hill, South East London.

'Mr Glasscock came down originally to get away from the Zeppelin raids, and stayed at King Arthur's Hotel, out on the cliffs, and stayed there for several years in fact. Sir Robert Harvey ran the hotel in those days. It was a very elegant place, ladies in evening dress . . . people like Noel Coward stayed there.'

I asked her about her former employer.

'Despite all the public appearances and the sword ceremonies, in later years, he was basically a very retiring man, almost a recluse in fact. I've been told Eirenikon means House of Peace . . . and it was certainly that: a very beautiful and peaceful house. He would spend

. . . and the Japanese garden.

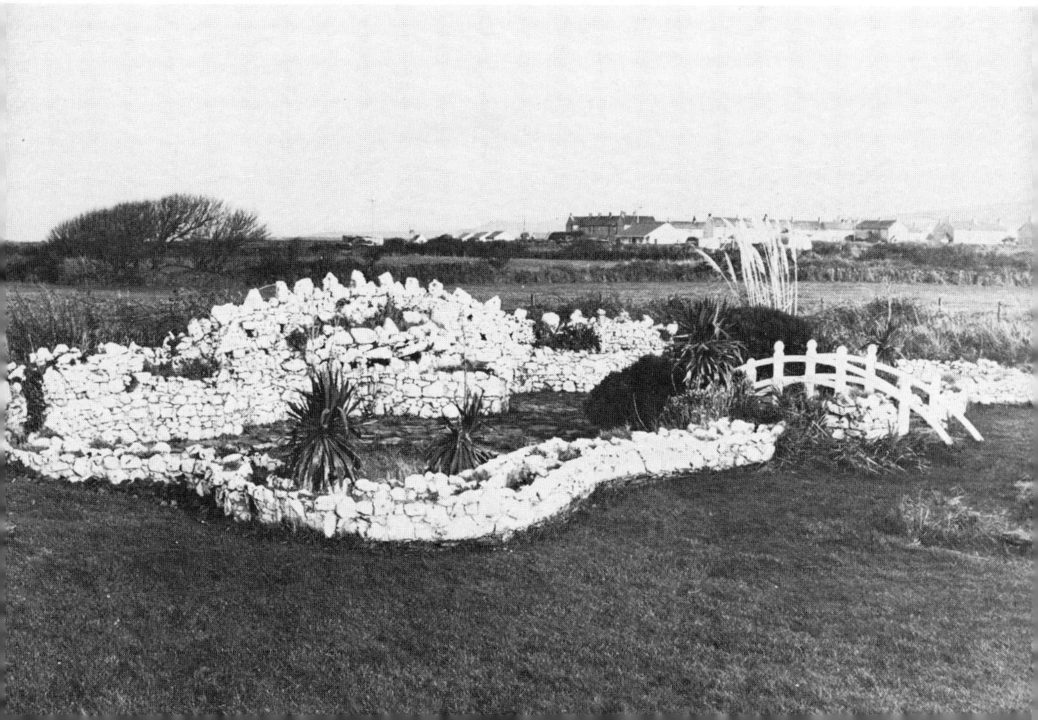

hours in the study and nobody would disturb him. If he and Eddie were discussing a business matter; nobody would go near the study, not even Mrs Glasscock.

'Yes, he was very firm, very strict, even to the extent of being a perfectionist. He wanted everything to be just right. But he was a most generous man. What he did for this village is nobody's business. He did a lot for the young people in particular. It was a terrible shock when we learnt that he had died on the liner and had been buried at sea.'

Today the Eirenikon, built in Edwardian style, is a residential home for the elderly. It stands in four and a half acres, just off the Bossiney Road. Sonia and I knew it in our Bossiney days when it was a hotel and motel run by Marcel Brodard, a cigar-smoking Frenchman and his English wife.

I shall always owe something to Frederick Thomas Glasscock, for his Hall of Chivalry helped to stimulate my interest in Arthurian matters, a vast and fascinating subject.

Open to the public during the season, the Hall remains an incredible monument to a complex character who clearly found his spiritual home here on the rugged North Cornish coast.

Peter Lanyon
Penwith

Peter Lanyon painted and exhibited in various countries. During the war he served in the Western Desert, Palestine and Italy. He crossed the Atlantic on a number of occasions, and visited Prague as a lecturer for the British Council.

Somebody once asked him, 'Do you see yourself as a national or international painter?'

'Neither,' he replied. 'I'm only a painter of the parish!'

His roots were firm in Penwith, and not simply in the soil. He was addicted to the sea, sky, the history, extracting enormous energy from the *whole* place.

I met him only half-a-dozen times, but he made a great impact.

Peter Lanyon was born in St Ives in 1918, and apart from schooling and the war years and his trips abroad, he remained there until his death in 1964—the result of a gliding accident over Somerset—robbing Cornwall of her greatest painter since John Opie, at the age of 46.

He intensely disliked the term 'modern art', loathing labels and watertight compartments. 'Art is continuous,' he told me, 'the artist is constantly changing people's vision. I've been called a lot of things in my time, but I see myself in the tradition of Constable, Turner, Nash and Cotman. The language I use is strange and is therefore called abstract.'

I once asked him, 'Which of your paintings have given you the greatest satisfaction?'

He almost dismissed the question.

'None of them! Why I've only scratched the surface, but I think I'm improving.' This was the height of his fame in the '60s, only a couple of years before he died. 'When it comes to looking at my own work, I feel really scared. I creep up on them. One day visiting a friend's house, I saw a painting and said "I like that". It was something I had done several years ago. When a painting is completed, I rarely look at it again.'

He believed the painter must be prepared to suffer. 'Especially in his efforts to communicate and if you're prepared to suffer enough, you usually get through . . . and remember communication may end in somebody rejecting your picture, even burning the thing, but that doesn't matter—you've succeeded in communicating.'

I remembered those comments a few years later at the Plymouth City Art Gallery in Tavistock Road: his one-man exhibition had been touring the country.

'Must be the work of a sick man,' grumbled a philistine from the Northcountry. 'The kids could do better,' added his wife.

How Peter would have chuckled. 'At least I've communicated . . .'

Seeing his work for the first time since his death was a strange experience. Outside it was a blistering hot day: minis and sunglasses, sandals and open-necked shirts; pavements as hot as frying pans. But inside the gallery there was a cool peace and calm; organ-music, rising from downstairs, generated a church-like quality. Touring those two rooms—96 Lanyon paintings covered the walls—intensified the sense of loss: one of the greatest Cornishmen of all time gone.

He told me of the obsessive nature of painting. 'I never really switch off,' he said. 'I may be watching television or listening to some music, but mentally I am often still in the studio.'

'You want to paint a particular chair; you have to become that chair. You meet it walking up the street, dressed as a woman. You go along a country road and you see it growing out of a tree, and then, perhaps you will go down to Sennen to get away from it all, and there in the cove, you see that chair again. This time it's part of the wall of somebody's house.'

Of Peter Lanyon's paintings, the art critic Alan Bowness, now Director of the Tate, has written:

'To appreciate them it is no more essential to know the Cornish landscape than it is to have been to Oxford, Mississippi, to understand William Faulkner. Lanyon's essential concern is with fundamentals, and he has always expressed himself in a language that is

Right: Peter Lanyon, 'painter of the parish . . . His roots were firm in Penwith . . .'

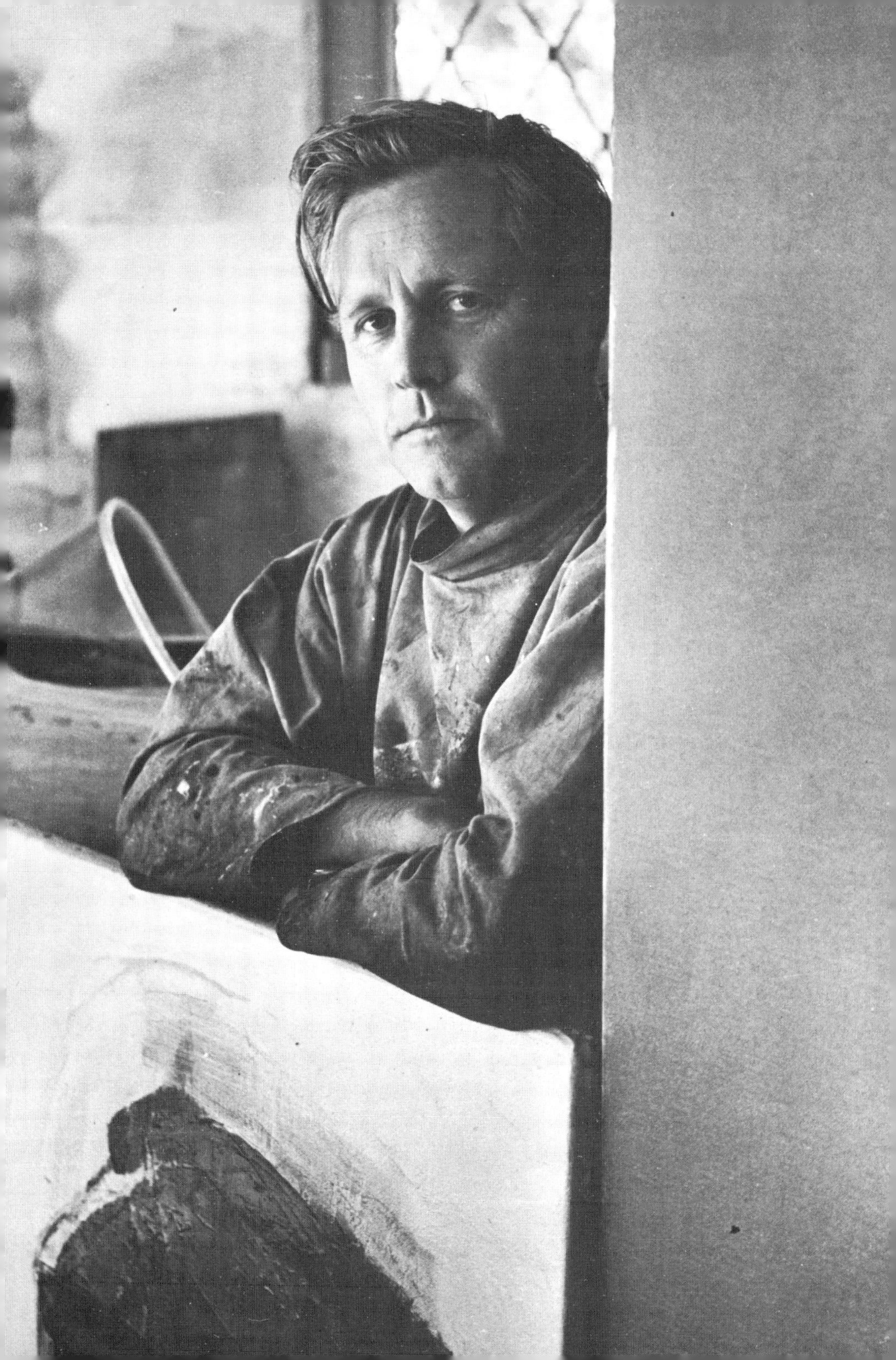

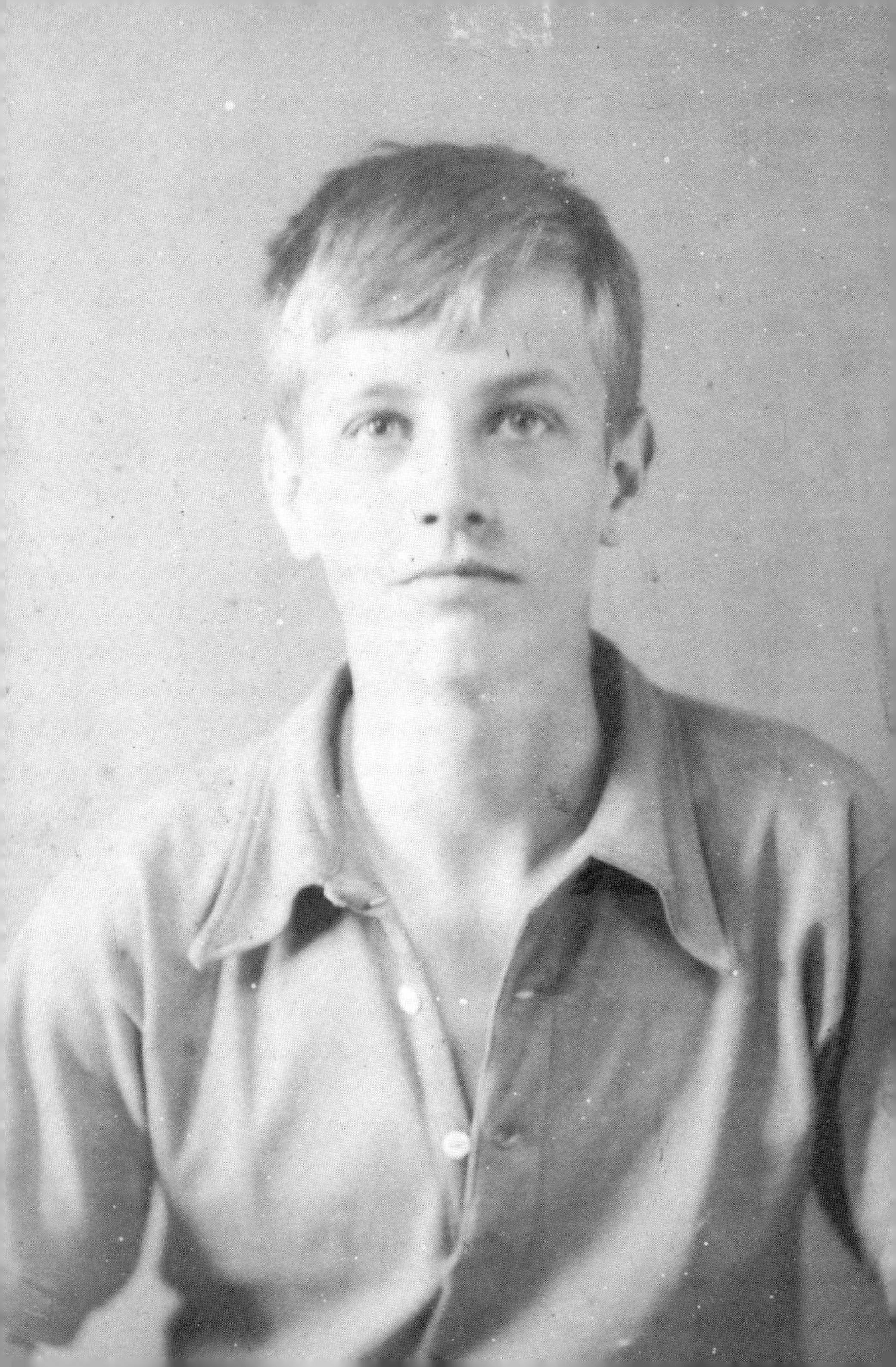

internationally comprehensible. As a painter his background is cosmopolitan . . .

'But Lanyon obstinately remains a painter of nature. For him landscape is not something we occasionally see, it is something we live in—the environment in which man naturally moves. To paint it, Lanyon needs to know his landscape intensely and completely, and this he does especially by physical activity. He delights in using mechanical means that were not available before the twentieth century: passing through the landscape at great speed, or hovering over it in a glider like a bird in flight, soaring and plunging, and all the while watching and feeling.'

In London, one wintery morning, I had an interesting experience visiting a Peter Lanyon one-man show with Danny Hall, an old cricketing friend who also happens to be an airline pilot. I was sometimes puzzled, but Danny knew instinctively what the artist was pinning to canvas. He felt a kindred spirit, looking down from the air, his eye sinking through the layers of colouring.

The strength of granite, the clarity of light, especially the brilliant Penwith light which brings out all those vibrant forms and colours, the rhythms of the Atlantic, the weather—that great 'English' pre-occupation—movements across and above the terrain, the meeting of sea and sky—these are only some of the beautiful Cornish images Peter Lanyon captured.

His first sense of Penwith journeys must have been as a small boy, in his father's motorcar, driving along that dramatic coastal road which curls and twists all the way from St Ives to Land's End.

He told me: 'I was blessed with my parents, both enlightened and both musical. They opened their home to friends on Sunday evenings for conversations on the arts and philosophy. I was lucky too in that my father got Borlase Smart to give me art lessons. Borlase Smart was this wonderful draughtsman, and I had the chance to visit local painters in their studios.'

Educated first at St Erbyn's School, Penzance, and then at Clifton, Peter Lanyon received formal art training in Penzance, and later in London at the Euston Road School.

'But the really important developments were my meetings with Ben Nicholson and Naum Gabo. I was doing a kind of painting

Left: Peter Lanyon in his youth.

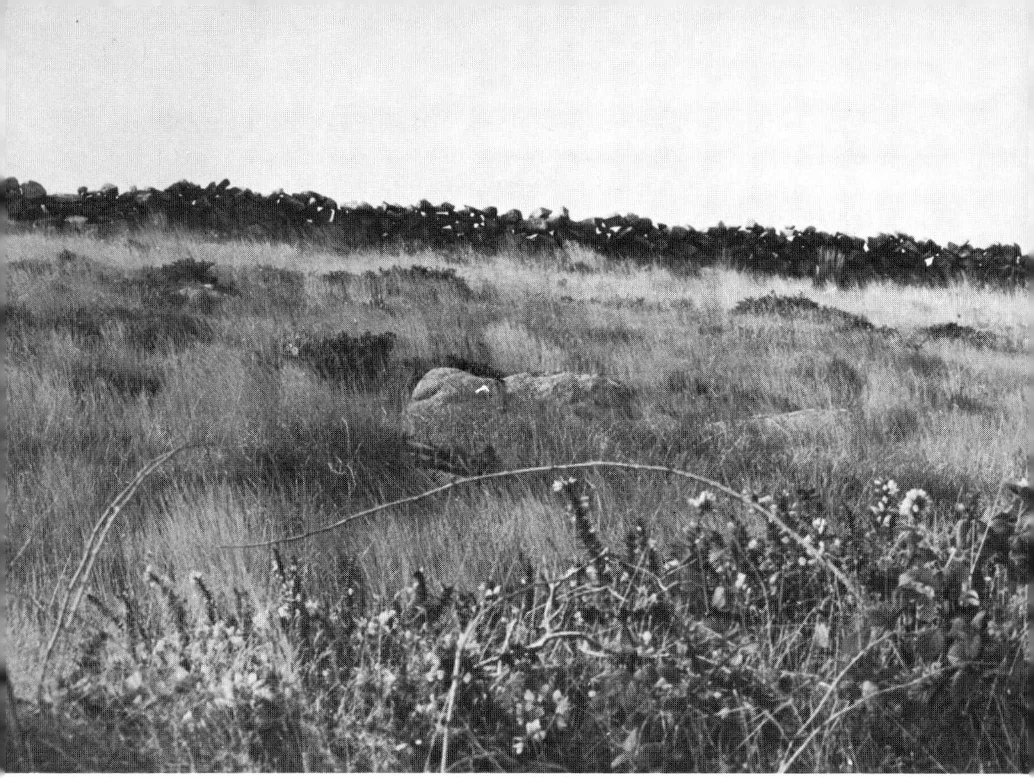

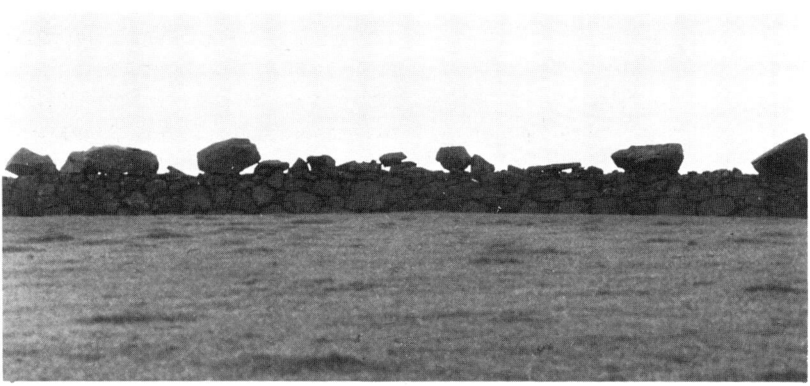

There is a strong sculptural quality in the landscape of Penwith—some of it man-made like these walls. They more than divide and define ownership, they make Penwith a place apart.

which most local people didn't understand and on meeting Nicholson I was thrilled to discover that he was working along the same lines, though obviously at a more advanced level. This fusion resulted in Nicholson giving me lessons for three or four months.

'That was all very valuable, but my meeting with the Russian Gabo made a deeper, more powerful impression . . . he was a more permanent influence.'

Peter Lanyon talked and wrote as vividly as he painted. It must now be a source of great regret he didn't commit more to paper. Here is how he defined the Cornishman in an article in *The Cornish Review* entitled 'The Face of Penwith'—no man or woman was better qualified to write such a theme or use such a title:

'The Cornishman is not double-faced, but multiple-faced, facets of character which add up to a sort of innocence. He is never still himself, except in death, but all the conflicts which lead to a game of hide and seek between native and the so-called 'foreigner' are part of a process which constantly surfaces the most diverse and conflicting factors. The Cornishman is fond of private secrets. A solemn intercourse of native with native, often intimate, is mistaken for a gossiping and vicious moralizing. The bush telegraph which puts the GPO to shame is a part of this game which is revealed to the unfortunate "foreigner". It is that part which concerns him alone, the rest is none of his business. Prayer is a strong force, and in the greatest days of revivalist services, in Wesleyan chapels, a poetic resolution was achieved. The loss of such inspiring services is as sad for Cornwall as the closing of the mines.'

Later in the same feature, he wrote about a favourite area of Penwith. For a Cornishman, an 'insider', he wrote with remarkable detachment—and he probably painted with the same detachment.

'From Wicca to Levant, the coastline emerges out of carns and bracken, and cultivated greenland, revealing on its varied faces a sea history and a land history of men within and without and a commerce of man with the weather. Here, in the small stretch of headland, cove and Atlantic adventure, the most distant histories are near the surface as if the final convulsion of rock upheaval and cold incision, setting in a violent sandwich of strata, had directed the hide and seek of Celtic pattern. A motor boat in some solemn gaiety with insistent cough, searches out the exacted payment of ocean on land; the small rituals of business at the junction of rock and sea wall.

Carn Galva: its great serrated crest is one of the most awe-inspiring sights in Cornwall. Ray Bishop's photograph shows too the stretch of dramatic moorland known as Hannibal's Carn. It's a magical place, yet curiously rarely found on the published page. But Peter Lanyon often glided over it, deriving great energy and inspiration from it all.

‘On carns of Zennor, Hannibal and Galva, where giants may have hurled their googlies in mild recreation, an outline of earthwork makes evidence for a primitive brotherhood of man, of the great and small in life and death, wherein animal joy and terror found resolution in the protective care of monolith and fort. Hereabouts, perhaps, the sun set westwards shifting down the monolith to bury the light of primitive fire and rose again in the hearts of men from the east. The saints were in Cornwall.

‘From Levant to Wicca, an easterly direction, chimneys are crowned by brick flourish, and the towers are lichen-covered, castellated and pinnacled. They rise upward out of the horizontal ground, as if the thrust of stone had surfaced to the call of the native, given up its wealth to his endeavour, and been revealed by manufacture as an expression of inner intent. Invention, leading to extension of native culture, made present in time a process of ancient development. The craft and skill and meaning of the native journey are outward and revealed at the land surface.’

He was kind enough, one Saturday morning in St Ives, to take me on a conducted tour of his one-man exhibition held in the town: a memorable morning, culminating in lunch in a St Ives bar and lots of good talk.

How I wished I had had a taperecorder and got more of his wisdom down. After that particular meeting, I started looking at the Cornish landscape with a different pair of eyes. Peter talked of how the landscape spoke back to him when he had captured the character or a feature in a painting. From that Saturday, I learnt that the landscape does, in fact, speak to us—provided we’re both humble and receptive.

Above all, he made me realise the landscape is not just something we see, but something we *live* in and *experience.*

It was more than a lesson. It helped to change my whole outlook. But then Peter Lanyon was that kind of man.

Wallace Nichols
Penzance

'See you when I'm next down in Penwith.'

'I'll look forward to that,' said the little man in the black beret and raincoat standing by the white gate.

It was a sombre afternoon: a grey sky and light ebbing from it and all around us rain dripping from the trees.

'Maybe then I'll talk you into coming to visit us at Bossiney.'

'Perhaps.' A faint smile creased his pale face as he waved 'good-bye' and I drove up the muddy lane. At the lodge I joined the Heamoor to Penzance road; coming face-to-face with the solid cemetery wall I turned right and into the town.

Unfortunately there was no next time. A few weeks later inside a copy of *The Cornishman* I saw his photograph and read his obituary. At 79, Wallace Nichols had died where he would have wished—at home.

Who was Wallace Nichols?

It is a difficult question. Wallace himself would have put those delicate fingers together, peered into the fire and simply said: 'A poet'. A poet he certainly was; a Georgian poet, one of the last of the breed, for he succeeded Masefield. But he was a subtle, several-sided character, the author of more than sixty books. Historical novelist, detective short-story writer, boys' adventure-book author and essayist—he would have cringed at the word journalist—he was also an authority on the speaking of verse.

The tragedy was fashion passed him by. He could not—or would not—alter his style or approach. Critics ignored him and local people knew little of his reputation. 'I don't suppose a dozen people in the

Right: Wallace Nichols, poet of Penzance, author of more than sixty books.

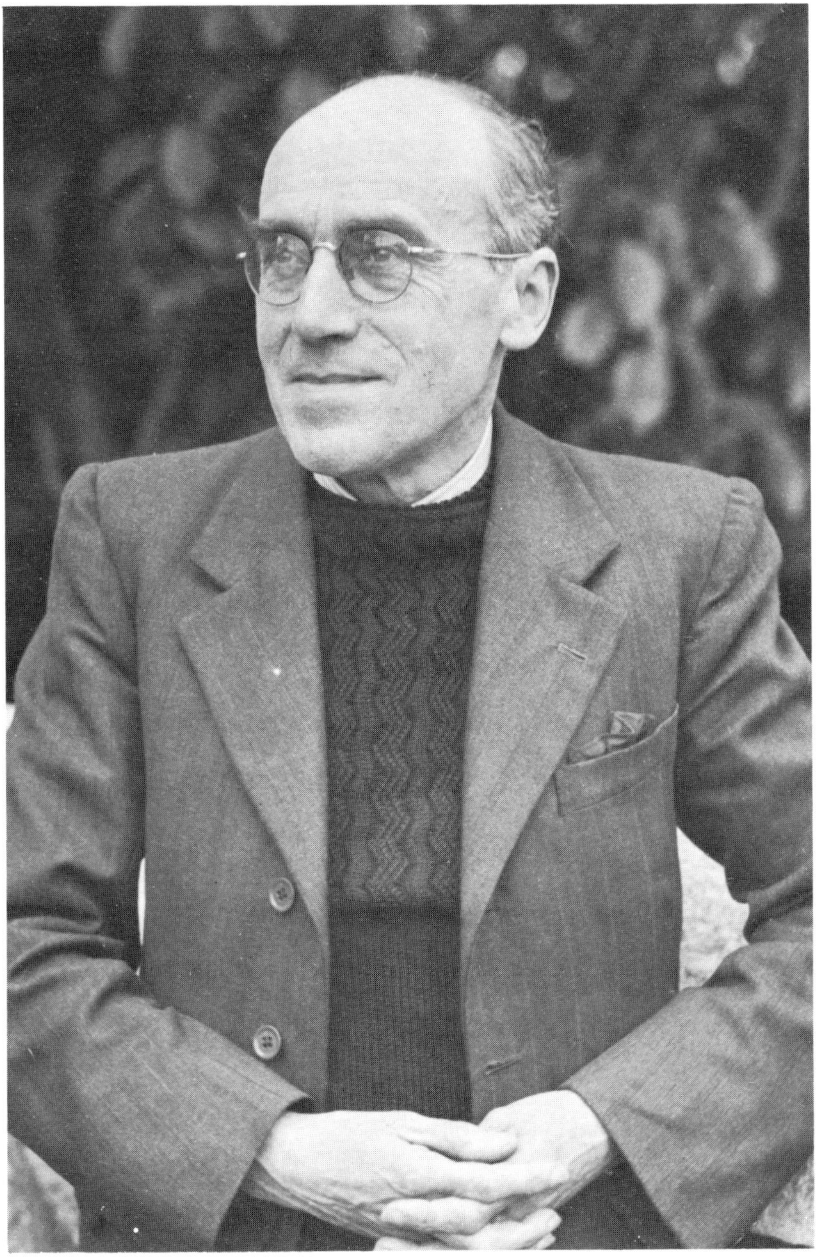

whole population of Penzance have read a book of mine,' he once confessed.

He lived his last years alone, at Usticke Haven, a house on the outskirts of Penzance dating from Elizabethan times, standing behind Nancealverne, the former home of Judge J. W. Scobell Armstrong, his only companion his dog—no television set, but a telephone and a radio which he called 'the wireless'.

I had the good fortune to spend numerous happy, informative hours with him there, either in the small panelled sitting room, seated in Shelley's chair, or downstairs in a room where he wrote and cooked and ate his meals. Sometimes in good weather we strolled through the grounds of Nancealverne: a beautiful little world of its own and with a lake and terrace; a wood and orderly stretches of lawn. I never saw him in a pair of shoes, only sandals or gum boots if there had been rain. Only once did I see him hurry and that was when a straying dog was about to 'desecrate' a lawn.

An hour in the company of Wallace Nichols was never dull or wasted. He was full of anecdotes. He had met Churchill and Elgar;

Another view from above: looking down on to Zennor with the Atlantic beyond.

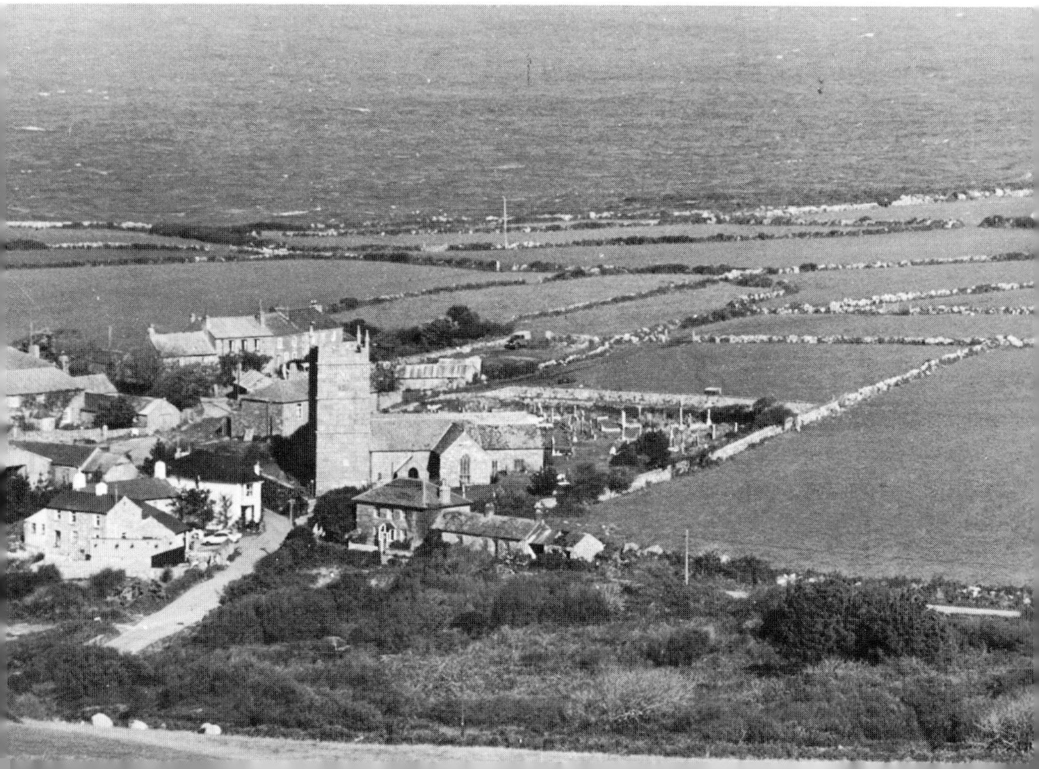

Dylan Thomas and Lawrence of Arabia. He could and should have written a brilliant autobiography. He tried but the manuscript came back with rejection slips. He spoke five modern languages and several obscure ones, including Egyptian and Babylonian. In conversation he coped with an impediment yet when he read you a piece of poetry the hesitations vanished. Clarity and confidence growing, ultimately taking over, his voice suddenly, surprisingly deepening, he would reveal the beauty and the meaning of every line. His text book of verse was dedicated to Edith Evans 'who can speak poetry perfectly', and was referred to by one young pro. as 'my professional bible'. Yet in the years I knew him only one Cornish amateur turned to him for help.

Wallace Nichols was, in some respects, the most extraordinary man I have ever known.

We first met about thirty years ago, finding ourselves sitting in an empty pavilion at the St Clare ground, facing a deserted cricket field, waiting for a cancelled match that was never due to begin: an ironic little episode, the only spectators at a non-event. Our next conversation was nearly a decade later. He was still wearing his black beret and sandals. I recalled our earlier meeting. He hadn't remembered but added: 'I'm not surprised that we should have met on a cricket ground because it's the only sport I'm interested in, the only game I've played.'

He thought it logical that cricket should have fired more poetry than any other sport. 'Cricket's clear-cut technique gives it a beauty which football can never attain. There seems something peculiarly aesthetic in the subject of a cricket team in action: the white and the green colourings and the rhythmical movement of the bat. I feel there is something almost Hellenic about a cricket match.' As a boy he had seen W. G. Grace bat. 'Later as the sub-editor of a London magazine I helped Jack Hobbs to correct proofs of his articles. I found him the most modest of the well-known men I've met and it embarrassed me when he persisted in calling me "sir"!'

It was John Page, then the editor of *The Cornishman*, who was responsible for our second meeting. I had been doing a fair amount of freelance work for his newspaper and suggested a series of articles on the writers in West Cornwall—and he had readily agreed.

Wallace Nichols happened to be the nearest—and consequently launched the series to the consternation of one local author who exclaimed: 'Fancy opening with a bloody lightweight!' Another

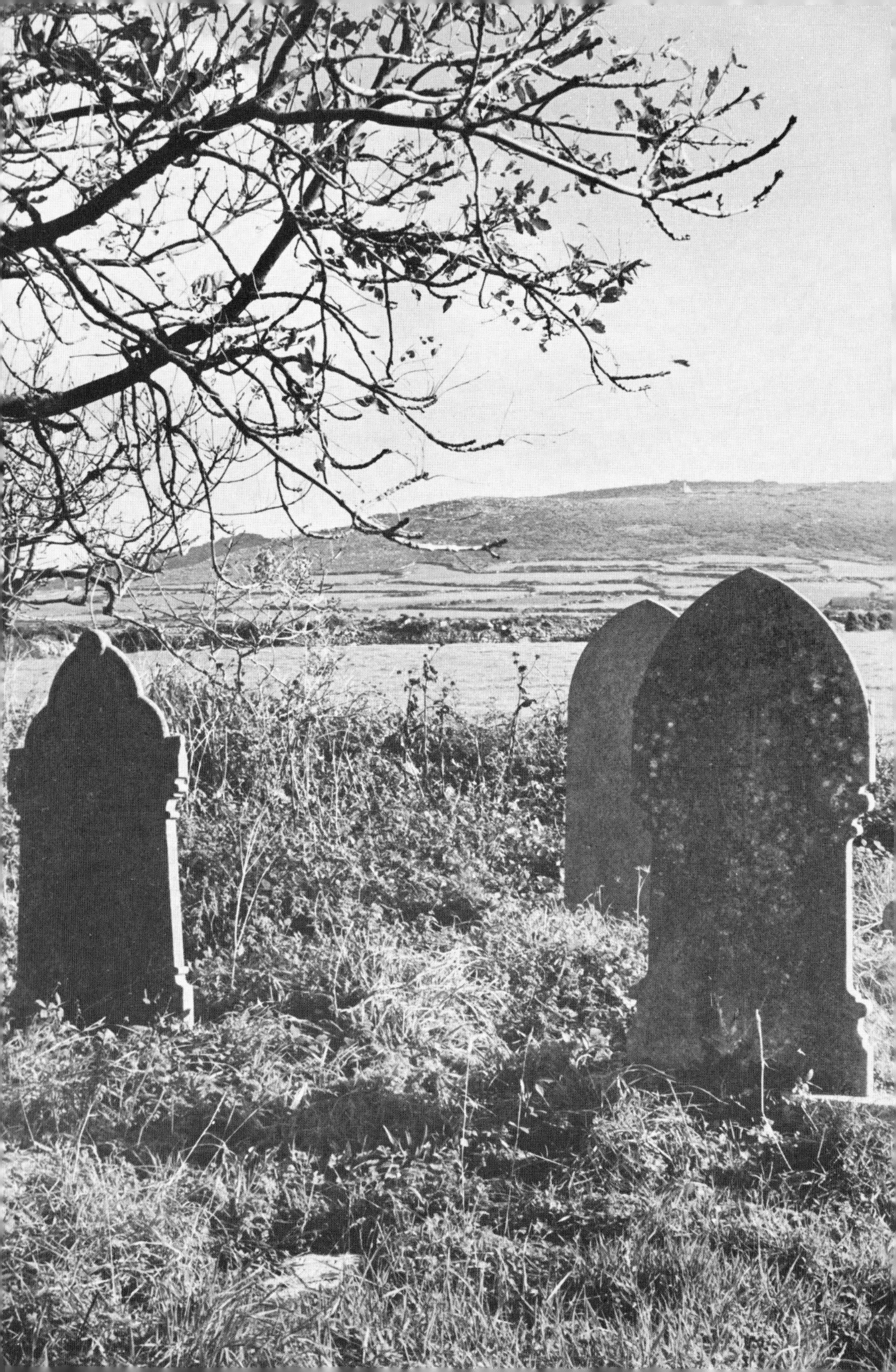

cynically observed: 'It's the first time I have heard of the little gentleman.' Wallace *was* a gentleman and he was on the short side, but I was less sure about 'the bloody lightweight' bit. The more I delved into his background, the more I read, the more I realised that he was being underestimated.

Of his *Laodice*, a play in three acts, *The Manchester Guardian*—as it then was—said: 'It is written in blank verse which is at times almost Shakespearian,' and *The News Chronicle* maintained: 'Mr Nichols has certainly done a fine thing in the writing and construction of this play; much of his verse has a lyric beauty as pure as it is memorable.'

The Scotsman, reviewing his selected lyrical poems, thought them: 'Worthy to be compared with Keat's *Nightingale* but, to a modern reader, more satisfying.'

William Kean Seymour, writing in *The Poetry Review*, described his *Saga of Judas* as 'one of the most ambitious poems of our decade, with a Miltonic thoroughness of conception . . .' and *The Times Literary Supplement* said: 'Mr Nichols has a grand sweep of imagination and a sonorous musical gift that urge his thoughts into exciting, resonant imagery.'

Peter Belloc, in his column in *The Daily Sketch*, called him 'one of the best historical novelists of our time', and across the Atlantic a critic referred to his short stories, featuring Sollius, the Roman slave detective, as 'the best since Sherlock Holmes'.

I approached our press interview with some anxiety. Naturally I wanted the series off to a good start, but I was very conscious of the impediment in his speech, his natural shyness, the fact that the greater part of half a century separated us and the realisation that the press, in recent years, had not always been kind to him.

John Osborne's central character in his play *West of Suez* says: 'You can never win an interview if you are being interviewed.' That may be so, but as one who has done his share of interviewing I have never believed in employing the proverbial knife, either in the physical encounter or later sitting at my typewriter. Anyway the

A rare angle: the Penwith landscape seen from Morvah Churchyard, one of the loveliest and sometimes least publicised parishes in all West Cornwall.

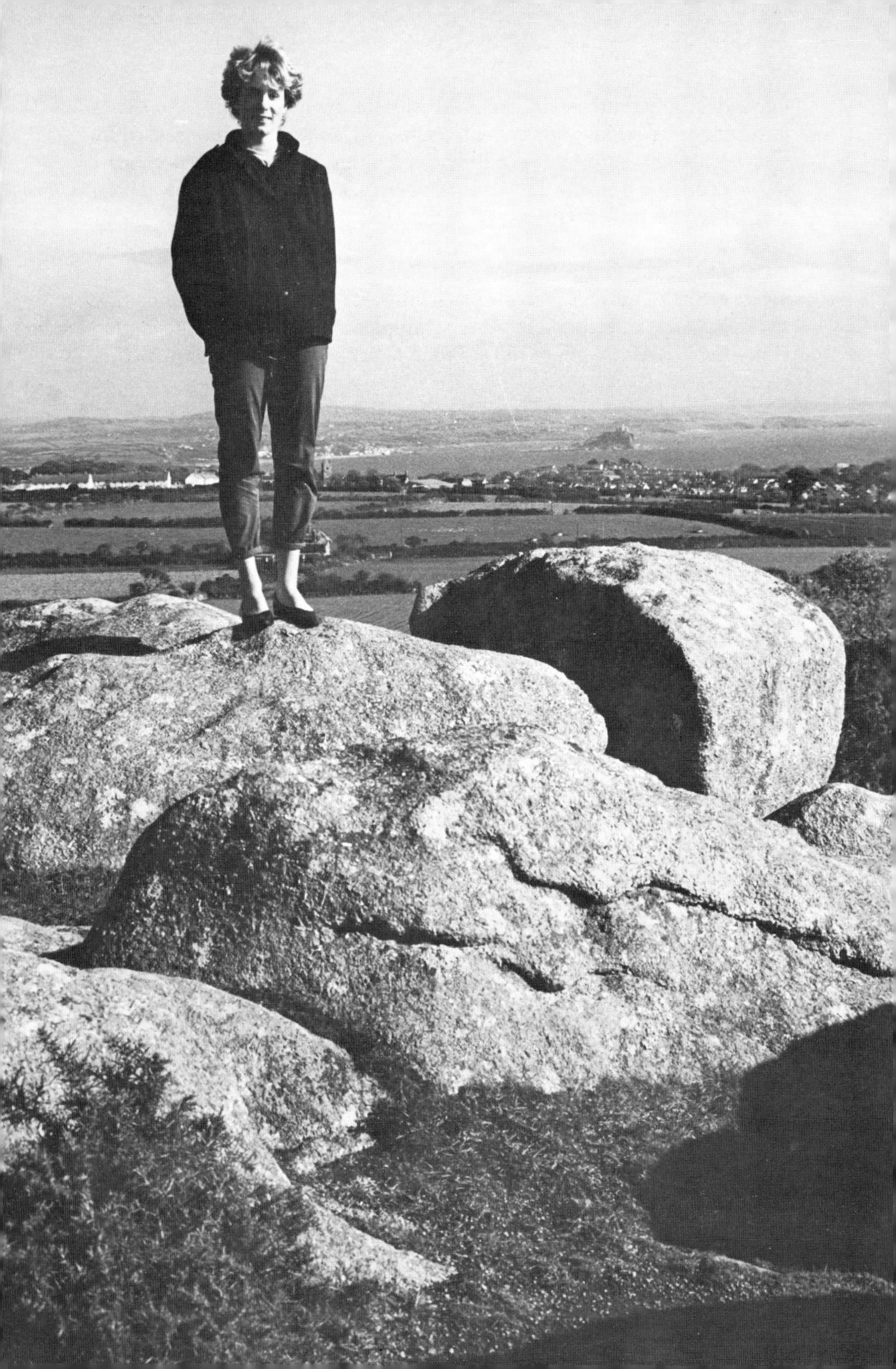

fears were groundless. Wallace, despite his occasional stumblings in mid sentence, turned out to be a perfect interviewee, and little did I realise as we toured the grounds that balmy September afternoon that the seeds of a friendship were being sown. For the next three years I saw him at least once a week, and sometimes more often; and when I later moved to Bossiney I never came westward without calling at Usticke Haven.

Getting to know Wallace though was no sudden happening. There was a certain iceberg quality, nothing forbidding but the knowledge that the greater part of his personality was unseen, unknown. Though he talked freely about literature, art and the theatre, he was basically shy. For the first year, he never called me 'Michael' and invariably began his letters 'Dear Michael Williams', yet in terms of friendship he was kindness itelf, helpful and encouraging. He was clearly very lonely and I like to think my visits to Usticke Haven helped him. Occasionally I would find him in some deep dark valley that was almost despair. 'How I wish I were your age,' he would sometimes say. His lack of material rewards and advancing years plagued him, and I sensed an unmentioned dread of ending up in an old people's home.

His wife, who came from French aristocracy, had died some years before. His dog Greto, though highly strung and capable of turning on his master now and then, was a great source of companionship. Wallace, for his part, was always neatly turned out but he lived and wrote in a state of chaos. His large writing table in the downstairs room, rather like those you found in old-fashioned farmhouse kitchens, was a constant mountain of paper: years old magazines, yellowed newspaper cuttings, dusty books, bills and letters.

In these last years I believe he found it hard to make ends meet. There had been some difficulty about insurance stamps and he was without a pension. We never discussed these matters at length. Nor did we discuss the woman in his life, though he dropped the occasional hint. In winter he was able to manage only the most meagre fires and I would sit in an overcoat listening to Wallace expounding on say the acting of Henry Irving, his hands outstretched over a few lumps of coal or a single bar of electricity.

'. . . one feels near the beginning of things on a Cornish moor.'

The poet, by nature, generally is a remote figure. Somebody once wisely reflected that those, waiting to see the light, must retire to the shadows. Wallace personified that: for ever in the wings, reluctant to take the stage. One of the kindest, most modest men ever to cross the Tamar, he was unfortunately the world's worst PRO, incapable of selling himself or his work.

Born in Birmingham in 1899, and educated at Westminster, his first book of poems was published at the age of sixteen. Sub-editor of *The Windsor Magazine* from 1914 to 1920, he became a publisher's reader for Ward, Lock & Co. Then, for health reasons, he came to Cornwall in 1934. His wife was appointed Curator of the Newlyn Art Gallery, a post she held until her death.

Despite all the disappointments and neglect, Wallace incredibly kept writing day after day—in memory's eye I can see him slightly round shouldered, a frail figure bent over his aged typewriter. *The London Mystery Magazine* regularly published his Roman slave detective stories—what a magnificent TV series they would have made—and Dobsons produced a string of fine boys' adventure stories, all I think set in Cornwall. Near the end—sadly a little too late—Derek Parker, a friend, became the editor of *The Poetry Review* which gave a new outlet for his poetry.

Cornwall? I once asked him about her influence.

'Cornwall's aura of the past,' he said, 'it certainly stimulates the writer's imagination. If you go through Madron village towards the open moors beyond, you are on the edge of prehistoric country, filled with the memories and memorials of a lost race . . . one feels near the beginning of things on a Cornish moor. For my part, the triangle formed by lines drawn from Madron to Morvah thence to Zennor and back to Madron, is the most wildly magical area of West Cornwall and I would willingly surrender any of the coves and beaches for its astringent beauty. The atmosphere of Cornwall has helped my imagination . . . even when not writing about the county. But really the writer—he should be able to write anywhere.'

If there is something beyond the grave, then I know this much: Wallace Nichols will be there writing away; wearing a black beret and sandals, and, of course, writing the first draft in his spidery longhand.

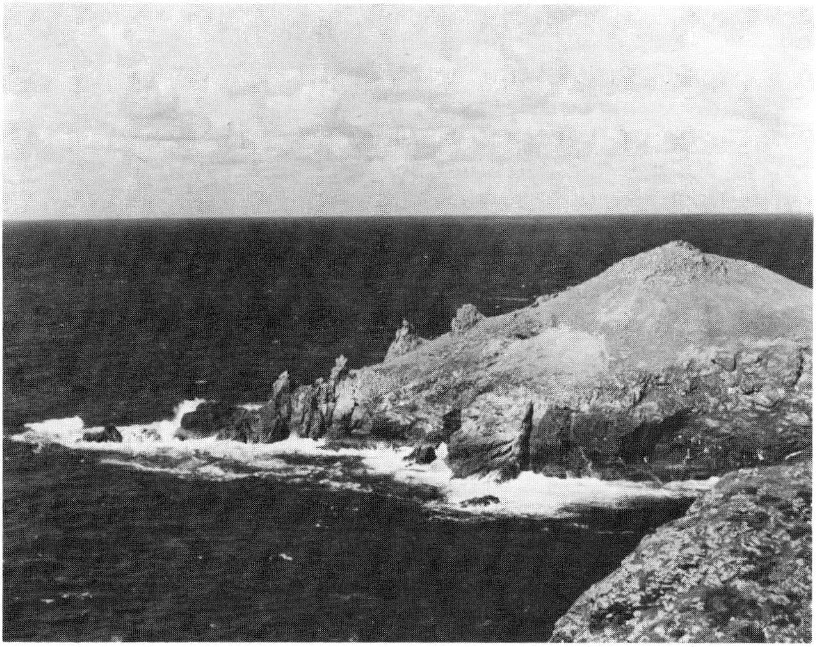

'The atmosphere of Cornwall has helped my imagination . . .'

ALSO AVAILABLE

100 YEARS ON BODMIN MOOR

by E V Thompson. 145 photographs.
A rich harvest of old photographs and picture postcards, reflecting life on the Moor for a century with perceptive text.
'*... timely that such a publication and collection of photographs should appear now, as a record for all of those who have loved and been inspired by Bodmin Moor.*'

Sarah Foot, The Western Morning News

RIVERS OF CORNWALL

by Sarah Foot. 130 photographs, 45 in colour.
The author explores six great Cornish rivers: the Helford, the Fal, the Fowey, the Camel, the Lynher and the Tamar.
'*... makes use of many colour illustrations as well as black and white and shows that whatever changes may have taken place in the river economics they remain places of quality and beauty, quintessentially Cornwall.*' The Cornish Guardian

AROUND LAND'S END

Michael Williams explores the end and the beginning of Cornwall. Wrecks and legends, the Minack Theatre, Cable & Wireless, Penwith characters and customs, lighthouses and Lyonesse all feature. 90 photographs, many of them from Edwardian and Victorian times, help to tell the story.
'*... a delightful stroll not only along the lanes but the legends of this celebrated area.*'

The Cornishman

MOUNT'S BAY

by Douglas Williams
More than 120 old photographs of an area stretching from Land's End to the Lizard with perceptive text by one of Cornwall's most respected journalists.
'*... a fascinating and exhaustive study ... It is a guidebook, potted history, pictorial gallery of Cornish life—all these things and very much more.*'

The Western Evening Herald

ECCENTRICS

by June Lander
With an introduction by Colin Wilson, June Lander has interviewed living people on the admission that they are eccentric.
'*... fascinating details about the lifestyles ... are bound to ensure another success for Bossiney.*' Cornwall Courier